Contributions to Management Science

More information about this series at http://www.springer.com/series/1505

Aswini Kumar Mishra • Ajay S. Vinzé
Rajorshi Sen Gupta • Rammohan Menon
Editors

Advances in Innovation, Trade and Business

Evidence from Emerging Economies

 Springer

Editors
Aswini Kumar Mishra
Department of Economics
BITS Pilani, K K Birla Goa Campus
Sancole, Goa, India

Ajay S. Vinzé
Trulaske College of Business
University of Missouri
Columbia, MO, USA

Rajorshi Sen Gupta
Department of Economics
BITS Pilani, K K Birla Goa Campus
Sancole, Goa, India

Rammohan Menon
Department of Economics
Birla Institute of Technology and Science
Goa, India

ISSN 1431-1941   ISSN 2197-716X   (electronic)
Contributions to Management Science
ISBN 978-3-030-60353-3   ISBN 978-3-030-60354-0   (eBook)
https://doi.org/10.1007/978-3-030-60354-0

This Springer imprint is published by the registered company Springer Nature Switzerland AG
The registered company address is: Gewerbestrasse 11, 6330 Cham, Switzerland

Preface

This volume comprises of papers by leading academicians, scholars and practitioners from India and abroad on current topics that are relevant to Innovation, Trade and Business. The experience from both economically developed and developing economies indicates the importance of innovation and trade. There seems to be ever-increasing importance of innovation leading to sustained growth of firms and industries. Moreover, trade creates expanded production and consumption opportunity of the nations. Thus, this volume intends to bring together the inter-related topics related to impact and determinants of innovation and trade across various geographic regions. This volume relates to various topics related to in the domain of international trade, investment and innovation in India and abroad.

The first chapter by P. Shankar presents a critical analysis of trade flows using a 'new trade decomposition' framework based on productivity analysis. Trade growth is decomposed into input, technological, efficiency effects and random effects. The paper develops a reforms evaluation framework for assessing the role of reforms in influencing the trade growth components.

In the second chapter, King David Kweku Botchway and Rajorshi Sen Gupta examine the causal link between foreign direct investment (FDI) and banking sector development (BSD) in French West Africa (FWA) and English West Africa (EWA) over the period 1990–2016. The results indicate a unidirectional Granger causality from BSD variables to FDI in both the regions. It is found that for English West Africa, there is bidirectional causality between private credit to GDP ratio and FDI. In the context of French West Africa, bidirectional causality is found between liquid liability ratio and FDI. The study emphasises the importance of strengthening financial sectors in attracting more FDI in underdeveloped countries.

In the third chapter, Sunil Kumar Ambrammal and Baiju P analyse the impact of FDI and TRIPS on the absorptive capacity of manufacturing firms in India. Using data from 44 sectors (Based on Department of Industrial Policy & Promotion) ranging from 2007 to 2017, they find that FDI led to enhancement in the absorptive capacity of Indian firms. There is, however, a negative impact of TRIPS on the absorptive capacity.

The fourth chapter by Pooja Verma examines the impact of Indian anti-dumping duties on import from the six ASEAN countries (Indonesia, Malaysia, Thailand, Singapore, Philippines and Vietnam) during the period 1995–2015. It is found that imports reduction from the ASEAN countries is significant due to the duties. However, the study finds insignificant trade diversion from non-named countries.

In Chap. 5, Abhishek Sinha, Aswini Kumar Mishra and Manogna RL analyse the determinants of performance of 'micro- and small-scale' firms vis-a-vis 'medium-scale' firms in seven manufacturing industry classifications for the period 2006–2017. At the aggregate level, firm performance is found to be significantly influenced by variations in firm size, firm age, raw material import intensity and capital intensity of firms. However, export intensity and R&D intensity are not found to significantly influence variations in firm performance. At the disaggregate level, the results indicate that firm performance is either insignificantly or negatively associated with R&D investment for micro and small firms. Export intensity is also not found to have a significant effect even at the industry level.

In Chap. 6, Rajarshi Mitra and Maria Evgenievna Guseva examine the link between population ageing and FDI inflows using Bayesian panel vector autoregressive model. Results show that in the context of OECD countries, there is no statistically significant relationship between population ageing and net FDI inflows. This is in stark contrast to the theoretical prediction of a negative relationship between population ageing and net FDI inflows.

Our seventh chapter by Manik Kumar analyses the productivity and efficiency of home-based enterprises in India using NSS data. It is found that total factor productivity growth of home-based enterprises is half of their counterparts. Nevertheless, total factor productivity growth of home-based enterprises has increased significantly during 2010–2011 to 2015–2016 when compared to previous period.

The eighth and final chapter of this volume by A.A.M. Nufile considers the impact of trade liberalisation implemented by Sri Lanka on the bilateral trade between Singapore and Sri Lanka. His empirics show that the free trade regime has been able to change the regional trade of Sri Lanka with Singapore after the liberalisation.

We are grateful to the authors for making their studies available for this edited volume. We sincerely hope that the studies included in this volume will stimulate academic debates and lead to further analytical advances in the domains of innovation and trade.

Goa, India   Aswini Kumar Mishra
Columbia, MO   Ajay S. Vinzé
Goa, India   Rajorshi Sen Gupta
Goa, India   Rammohan Menon

Acknowledgements

This Volume in Springer Series contains eight selected papers presented or accepted at the 2nd International Conference on Economics & Finance (ICEF-2020) held at Birla Institute of Technology and Science, Pilani-K K Birla Goa Campus, Goa, India, during Jan 23–25, 2020. The event aimed at stimulating critical thinking and sharing knowledge across emerging themes towards trade, business and innovation and related fields.

Eminent speakers like Jeffrey C. Thomson, President and CEO of IMA® (Institute of Management Accountants); Prof. Avanidhar (Subra) Subrahmanyam, Distinguished Professor of Finance, Goldyne and Irwin Hearsh Chair in Money and Banking, The John E. Anderson Graduate School of Management, University of California at Los Angeles (UCLA); Dr. Hamza Ali Malik, Director , Macroeconomic Policy and Financing for Development Division, United Nations Economic and Social Commission for Asia and the Pacific (United Nations ESCAP); Dr. Sweta Chaman Saxena, Chief, Macroeconomic Policy and Analysis, Macroeconomic Policy and Financing for Development, UN Economic and Social Commission for Asia and the Pacific (UN-ESCAP); Prof. Sanket Mohapatra, Economics Area Chairperson, IIM Ahmedabad; Prof. Sujeet K. Sharma, Associate Professor, Informations System & Analytics, IIM Trichy; Dr. Joyojeet Pal, Principal Researcher, Microsoft Research India; Prof. Prakash Singh, Professor in Finance & Accounting IIM, Lucknow; and Mr. Jaywardhan Semwal, Vice President, Corporate Financial Accounting, Hewlett Packard Enterprise delivered distinguished lectures on this occasion. The event was supported by National Bank for Agriculture and Rural Development (NABARD) and Institute of Management Accountants (IMA®) provided an avenue for disseminating information on contemporary research and future practices in economics.

An edited book such as this also required the cooperation and dedication of its many contributing authors. Apart from penning excellent chapters, the authors were always prompt in their responses. We are also indebted to the anonymous referees and members of scientific committee for providing insightful reviews with many useful comments and suggestions.

This book deserves mentioning of a few colleagues and research scholars whose indefatigable efforts helped us in compiling this book. We would particularly like to thank (in no particular order) for the help and cooperation received from Dr. Arfat Ahmad Sofi, Dr. Sukumar Vellakkal and Mr. Abhishek Kumar Sinha. We would also like to acknowledge the support we received from Prof. Raghurama G, Director, BITS Pilani-K K Birla Goa Campus, in organising the above-mentioned event, and this book is an outcome of it.

Most importantly, we would like to thank Springer editor, Nitza Jones- Sepulveda and Assistant Editor, Faith Su for their enthusiasm, advice, and encouragement.

Contents

1   Towards a New Framework for Analysing Trade
    Growth Dynamics   1
    Pragya Shankar

2   An Empirical Analysis of Foreign Direct Investment (FDI)
    and Banking Sector Development (BSD) in West Africa   35
    King David Kweku Botchway and Rajorshi Sen Gupta

3   Impact of FDI and TRIPS on the Absorptive Capacity
    of Manufacturing Firms in India   47
    Sunil Kumar Ambrammal and P. Baiju

4   The Trade Impact of Indian Anti-Dumping Measures
    on ASEAN-6 Countries   57
    Pooja Verma

5   Examining the Performance of MSME Firm in India:
    An Empirical Analysis at Industry Level   69
    Abhishek Kumar Sinha, Aswini Kumar Mishra, and R. L. Manogna

6   Does Population Ageing Reduce FDI Inflows in OECD
    Countries? Evidence from Bayesian Panel VAR Estimates   85
    Rajarshi Mitra and Maria Evgenievna Guseva

7   Productivity and Efficiency of Home-Based Enterprises
    in India: Evidence from NSS Data   95
    Manik Kumar

8   An Analysis of the Trade Relationship of Sri Lanka
    with Singapore Based on Trade Liberalization   123
    A. A. M. Nufile

Index   133

List of Figures

Fig. 4.1   India's export and import share with ASEAN-6 Ministry of
           Commerce & Industry of India (2018(b)) 61
Fig. 4.2   Trend of India's anti-dumping cases against ASEAN 6 imports .. 63

Fig. 5.1   Distribution of sample firms by industry classification 74
Fig. 5.2   Relationship between firm size and firm performance (ROA) 75
Fig. 5.3   Relationship between firm age and firm performance (ROA) 75
Fig. 5.4   Relationship between capital intensity and firm performance
           (ROA) 76
Fig. 5.5   Relationship between R&D Intensity and firm performance
           (ROA) 76
Fig. 5.6   Relationship between export Intensity and firm performance
           (ROA) 77

Fig. 6.1   Age-dependency ratio for the old in OECD 86
Fig. 6.2   Impulse response functions for bivariate model 1 93
Fig. 6.3   Impulse response functions for bivariate model 2 94

Fig. 7.1   Total factor productivity growth of home-based enterprises and its
           counterpart. 104
Fig. 7.2   Scale efficiency of home-based enterprises
           and its counterpart. 105
Fig. 7.3   Technical efficiency of home-based enterprises and its
           counterpart 105
Fig. 7.4   Estimated number of enterprises by enterprises type
           (in lakhs) by sector 116
Fig. 7.5   Real gross value-added per-enterprises
           by enterprises type 117
Fig. 7.6   Estimated number of worker by enterprises type 117
Fig. 7.7   Real value of fixed asset per-enterprises
           by enterprises type 117
Fig. 7.8   Estimated number of enterprises by category
           of enterprises 118

Fig. 7.9   Real gross value-added of enterprises by category
           of enterprises   118
Fig. 7.10 Real fixed asset of enterprises by category
           of enterprises   118
Fig. 7.11 Number of worker in enterprises by category
           of enterprises   119
Fig. 8.1   Sri Lanka's trade with Singapore (1980–2018)   128
Fig. 8.2   Singapore's trade with Sri Lanka (1980–2018)   128

List of Tables

Table 1.1	Coverage of various reform areas	9
Table 1.2	Variable definition	13
Table 1.4	Trade growth decomposition—developed countries (Figures in percentages)	15
Table 1.5	Trade growth decomposition—developing countries (Figures in percentages)	16
Table 1.3	Trade growth decomposition—full sample (Figures in percentages)	18
Table 1.6	Trade growth decomposition: developing countries and all partners (Figures in percentages)	19
Table 1.7	ICT—Trade growth decomposition (Figures in numbers (percentages in square brackets))	21
Table 1.8	IMPCOU—Trade growth decomposition (Figures in numbers (percentages in square brackets))	22
Table 1.9	NTB—Trade growth decomposition (Figures in numbers (percentages in square brackets))	23
Table 1.10	STABUS—Trade growth decomposition (Figures in numbers (percentages in square brackets))	24
Table 1.11	Frontier estimation, world trade flows, 2001	30
Table 1.12	Frontier estimation, world trade flows, 2007	31
Table 2.1	Definition of variables	38
Table 2.2	Hypotheses tested in this study	41
Table 2.3	Descriptive statistics	42
Table 2.4	Cross-sectional dependence test	42
Table 2.5	Panel unit root test	43
Table 2.6	Granger causality test	43
Table 3.1	Summary statistics of the variables	52
Table 3.2	Correlation matrix	52
Table 3.3	Joint effect of IPR and FDI on the ACAP	53
Table 3.4	Impact of FDI & IPR independently on ACAP	54

Table 4.1   India's top 10 AD targets (1995–2015), World Trade
            Organisation (2016) AntiDumping Initiations
            and Measures by Member Countries   58
Table 4.2   Summary of AD case against ASEAN-6 imports,
            Ministry of Commerce and Industry of India (2018(a))   62
Table 4.3   AD case by industries against ASEAN-6 (1995–2015)
            Ministry of Commerce and Industry of India (2018(a))   63
Table 4.4   Results of AD cases against named ASEAN-6 imports vs.
            not-named ASEAN and other vs. all countries   65
Table 5.1   Definition of variables   77
Table 5.2   Distribution of sample firms by industry classification   77
Table 5.3   Descriptive statistics of the variables   78
Table 5.4   Correlations matrix   78
Table 5.5   Fixed effects for firm performance   79
Table 5.6   Fixed effects model for ROA with industry grouping   81
Table 6.1   Panel unit root tests   90
Table 6.2   Bivariate Bayesian panel VAR estimates   91
Table 6.3   Multivariate bayesian panel VAR estimates   92
Table 7.1   Partial productivity by enterprises category 103
Table 7.2   Partial productivity of HBE by sector 106
Table 7.3   Total factor productivity and efficiency
            (scale and technical) of home-based enterprises
            by sector 107
Table 7.4   Partial productivity of HBE by ownership type 107
Table 7.5   Total factor productivity and efficiency
            (scale and technical) of home-based enterprises
            by type of ownership 108
Table 7.6   Partial productivity of HBE by social group of owner 109
Table 7.7   Total factor productivity and efficiency
            (scale and technical) of home-based enterprises
            by social group 109
Table 7.8   Partial productivity of HBE by subcontracting 111
Table 7.9   Total factor productivity and efficiency
            (scale and technical) of home-based enterprises
            who are working on subcontracting 112
Table 7.10 Partial productivity of HBE by type of subcontracting 112
Table 7.11 Total factor productivity and efficiency
            (scale and technical) of home-based enterprises
            by nature of subcontracting 113
Table 7.12 Partial productivity of HBE by industry groups 114
Table 7.13 Total factor productivity and efficiency
            (scale and technical) of home-based enterprises
            by industrial group 115

Table 8.1   Sri Lanka–Singapore bilateral trades (1980–2018)
             values in US $ million 127
Table 8.2   Regression results for the log–linear model of post-liberalization
             period (1980–2018) (influence factors on Sri Lanka–Singapore
             bilateral trade) 129

About the Editors

Aswini Kumar Mishra presently serves as the Head in the Department of Economics and an Associate Professor at BITS, Pilani-K K Birla Goa Campus, India. His research and teaching interests relate to applied econometrics, behavioural and industrial economics and financial risk management. Dr. Mishra has published related articles in most leading scholarly journals including *Global Business Review*, *International Journal of Technological Learning, Innovation and Development*, *International Journal of Business and Globalisation, Science, Technology and Society* and *Journal of Strategy and Management*.

Ajay S. Vinzé presently serves as Dean of the Robert J. Trulaske, Sr. College of Business, University of Missouri. Dr. Ajay Vinze's research has focused on data analytics, emergency preparedness and response, economic value of ICT investments and collaborative computing. His publications have appeared in most leading scholarly (Information System) journals including *Information Systems Research*, *MIS Quarterly*, *Decision Sciences*, *Decision Support Systems*, *Health Affairs* and various *IEEE* and *ACM Transactions*. Dr. Vinzé is a Fulbright Senior Specialist and has served on the faculty of the W. P. Carey School of Business, ASU, and the May School of Business, Texas A&M University.

Rajorshi Sen Gupta is an Assistant Professor of Economics at BITS Pilani KK Birla Goa Campus, India. He obtained his PhD from Texas A&M University, USA. His research interests encompass broad areas of Economics including Innovation and Intellectual Property Management, Principal-Agent contracts, Transportation economics and Economic problems of underdeveloped nations. He has worked at premier institutes like Texas Transportation Institute (USA), Indicus Analytics, National Institute of Public Finance and Policy, India. He has also received prestigious awards like Ford Foundation Scholarship and Tom Slick Fellowship for his research.

Rammohan Menon currently serves as a guest faculty for finance courses in the Department of Economics at BITS Pilani KK Birla Goa Campus, India. He is a Fellow of The Institute of Cost Accountants of India and a Certified Management Accountant of USA. Mr. Menon is very passionate about teaching. During his teaching career spanning over 25 years, he has taught various subjects in finance at leading institutes of Goa, India. He also possesses vast experience of 20 years in the corporate world at very senior and CEO levels. He has been a consultant and auditor for many companies in India. He has a long experience in the corporate world, expertise in multifarious areas of Finance and Accounting.

Contributors

Sunil Kumar Ambrammal Department of Humanities and Sciences, National Institute of Technology Goa, Goa, India

P. Baiju Department of Humanities and Sciences, National Institute of Technology Goa, Goa, India

King David Kweku Botchway Department of Economics, BITS-Pilani K K Birla Goa Campus, Goa, India

Rajorshi Sen Gupta Department of Economics, BITS-Pilani K K Birla Goa Campus, Goa, India

Maria Evgenievna Guseva Business Analytical Department, Central Bank of Russian Federation, Moscow, Russian Federation

Manik Kumar Centre for Budget and Governance Accountability, New Delhi, Delhi, India

R. L. Manogna Department of Economics, BITS Pilani, K K Birla Goa Campus, Goa, India

Aswini Kumar Mishra Department of Economics, BITS Pilani, K K Birla Goa Campus, Goa, India

Rajarshi Mitra Institute for International Strategy, Tokyo International University, Tokyo, Japan

A. A. M. Nufile Department of Economics and Statistics, South Eastern University of Sri Lanka, Oluvil, Sri Lanka

Pragya Shankar Ram Lal Anand College, Delhi University, New Delhi, India

Abhishek Kumar Sinha Department of Economics, BITS Pilani, K K Birla Goa Campus, Goa, India

Pooja Verma Department of Economics, Jamia Millia Islamia, New Delhi, India

Chapter 1
Towards a New Framework for Analysing Trade Growth Dynamics

Pragya Shankar

1.1 Introduction

Global development experience shows that no sizable country has sustained rapid economic growth (seven plus and above) without sustained export growth backed by appropriate trade policies (Acharya 2019; Roy 2019). According to World Bank (2018), strong open trade policies promote economic growth by accelerating innovation, productivity, income, opportunities and provision of affordable goods and services to low-income households. They also play a direct role in reducing global poverty. UN-DESA (2015) sums this as the relation between trade and structural transformation that is observed as the graduation of many countries out of LDC (Least Developed Countries) status.

Existing literature has analysed several aspects of trade dynamics and growth. Few of these are constant market share analysis (Jepma 1986), rank ordering of commodities and countries based on product cycle approach (Feenstra and Rose 1997), intensive and extensive margin approach (Evenett and Venables 2002; Hummels and Klenow 2005), decomposition using gravity model (Novy 2009) and decomposition based on stochastic frontier gravity models (Kalirajan 2010).

Kalirajan (2010) in his decomposition stresses on the interactions between trade growth dynamics, trade costs and reforms. He decomposes total exports growth of a country with its various trade partners countries into the sum of changes in demand and trade costs, with the latter being composed of 'explicit beyond the border barriers', 'implicit beyond the border barriers' and 'behind the border barriers'. Reforms are found to promote trade growth by reducing 'implicit beyond the border barriers'. This method is formulated for assessing trade growth of a particular

P. Shankar (✉)
Ram Lal Anand College, Delhi University, New Delhi, India

© The Author(s), under exclusive license to Springer Nature Switzerland AG 2021
A. K. Mishra et al. (eds.), *Advances in Innovation, Trade and Business*,
Contributions to Management Science,
https://doi.org/10.1007/978-3-030-60354-0_1

country with all its trade partners. Kalirajan and Khan (2011) apply it to analyse Pakistan's export growth between 1999 and 2004.

The above literature survey reveals one area of potential research, viz., of developing a trade growth decomposition framework based on the concepts of productivity analysis. Productivity analysis decomposes output growth into input effect, technological effect and efficiency effect. Both frontier and data envelopment analysis techniques have been used for this decomposition. This paper tries to develop a trade decomposition framework using the concepts from productivity analysis.

The relevance for such an exercise can be justified from the following observations: (i) Trade facilitation polices are found to increase trade by reducing trade costs (Wilson et al. 2004, Duval and Utoktham 2009, 2011a, 2011b and so on). This corresponds to the concept of 'input effect' in productivity analysis; (ii) Berkowitz et al. (2006) have applied the Trade Facilitation and Export Competitiveness framework outlined in Spence and Karingi (2011) to develop the concepts of production and transaction effects. These effects measure the impact of change in export productivity on trade growth. The sum of these two effects, technological effect, is related to the technological effect used in output growth decomposition (Kumbhakar and Bhaumik 2010); and (iii) The efficiency effect documented in Stochastic Frontier Gravity Models (Armstrong et al. 2008; Kalirajan and Khan 2011) is the counterpart of efficiency effect in productivity analysis.

Thus, existing literature reveals a close correspondence between aspects of trade and output growth dynamics. The next step in this direction would be to develop a quantitative model that can represent all aspects of trade growth, as found for output growth.

The starting point for this proposed model is Kumbhakar and Bhaumik (2010). The authors develop an output growth decomposition framework by taking the difference of two cross-sectional stochastic frontier production models (estimated for a point in time). Analogous to Kumbhakar and Bhaumik (2010), the proposed model is obtained by taking the difference of two cross-sectional stochastic frontier gravity models. Four terms are identified in this trade growth decomposition: input effect, technological effect, efficiency effect and random effect. While the first three are analogous to components found in output growth decomposition (Kumbhakar and Bhaumik 2010), the fourth, a new term, captures the effect of random shocks on trade growth. Interpretation of model terms is as based on the above-mentioned literature.

Next step in this modelling is hypotheses on trade growth patterns. UNIDO (2005) and Kumbhakar and Bhaumik (2010) discuss expected patterns of output dynamics for developed and developing countries. This literature is used to develop hypotheses on expected trade growth patterns of developing and developed countries.

Finally, keeping up with Kalirajan (2010), a new method for assessing the role of reforms in influencing trade dynamics is proposed.

The model contributes to the existing literature in the following ways: (i) it provides a new method for analysing trade growth dynamics and of reforms in influencing trade growth; and (ii) provides for comparison with output growth. This can provide a deeper understanding of processes involved in structural transformation and development, as discussed by World Bank (2018) and UN-DESA (2015) above.

The paper is structured as follows: Sect. 1.2 lists the objectives of this paper. Section 1.3 discusses the data description and methodology. Section 1.4 presents the results, while Sect. 1.5 concludes.

1.2 Objectives

1. Develop a trade growth decomposition model based on concepts of productivity analysis for analysing trade growth of countries/regions. Trade growth decomposed into input effect, technological effect, efficiency effect and random effect.
2. Develop a reforms evaluation framework for assessing role of reforms in influencing trade growth.

1.3 Data and Methodology

1.3.1 Data Description

This paper builds a trade growth decomposition model using stochastic frontier inverse gravity model and uses it to describe trade growth patterns of developing and developed countries. It also investigates the role of reforms in this process. Data for undertaking these analyses are taken from the following sources.

A total of 34 countries constituting a sample of 1097 bilateral merchandize trade flows are used for estimating frontier models for the years 2001 and 2007. These countries featured in the list of top 50 exporters for the years 2001 and 2007 (WTO 2008) and accounted for about 75% of world merchandize trade in these years.

The Global Competitiveness Report, GCR, released by World Economic Form and Harvard University (2010) divides these 34 countries into five categories according to their level of development:

Stage 1: Low developed, factor driven countries (Bangladesh (**Bgd**), India (**Ind**));
Transition from Stage 1 to Stage 2: (Philippines (**Phl**), Vietnam (**Vnm**));
Stage 2: Efficiency driven economies (China (**Chn**), Colombia (**Col**), Indonesia (**Idn**), South Africa (**Zaf**), Sri Lanka (**Lka**) and Thailand (**Tha**));
Transition from Stage 2 to Stage 3: (Argentina (**Arg**), Brazil (**Bra**), Chile (**Chl**), Malaysia (**Mys**), Mexico (**Mex**), Romania (**Rom**), Russia (**Rus**) and Turkey (**Tur**));
Stage 3: Innovation driven economies or frontier countries (Australia (**Aus**), Austria (**Aut**), Belgium (**Bel**), Canada (**Can**), France (**Fra**), Germany (**Deu**), Israel

(**Isr**), Italy (**Ita**), Japan (**Jpn**), Korea (**Kor**), Netherland (**Nld**), Spain (**Esp**), Sweden (**Swe**) , Switzerland (**Che**), GBR (**UK**), USA (**US**)).

Trade frontier countries like Singapore and Hong Kong have been excluded due to data limitations.

Data for the dependent variable of the inverse gravity equation has been collected from the earlier version of **TRADE COSTS DATABASE.**

Data on gravity covariates, viz. bilateral distance, common border and common language, has been taken from **CEPII**. Membership in Free trade areas has been constructed using the list of FTA agreements given on the **WTO** Website. Domestic trade costs are represented using unadjusted (not chain linked) overall country scores from Annual Report of Economic Freedom Network (**EFN**), released by the Heritage Foundation.

Reform areas: Information and Communication Technology Expenditure is sourced from World Development Indicators. Reform areas measuring Tariff and Non-Tariff Barriers, Government's Business Start-Up Regulations, Import and Export Costs, Protection of Property Rights and Efficiency of Legal Framework for Settling Disputes and Challenging Legality of Government Actions are sourced from Economic Freedom Network (**EFN**).

Variables need not be adjusted for price changes as the dependent variable is in the form of a ratio (Novy and Chen 2009) and the independent variables are in the form of indices. No cases of multicollinearity are reported in the data set as the highest magnitude of variance inflation factor is found to be 3.19 (Model 3, Year 2001, Appendix 1 Table 1.11).

The estimation of the Frontier Models has been done using Stata 13 Software. Results provide observation-wise magnitudes of one-sided error term and predicted values, from which magnitudes of the two-sided error terms are obtained.

1.3.2 Methodology

The methodology in this analysis is explained under two parts. The first part explains the construction of the trade growth decomposition model and the reforms evaluation framework. Hypotheses on trade growth patterns and role of reforms on influencing trade growth are also reported. The second part reports the econometric model, the specification of the inverse frontier model, for this paper. Descriptive statistics of some key variables are also presented.

1.3.2.1   Trade Growth Decomposition and Reforms Evaluation: Concepts and Hypotheses

Trade Growth Decomposition: Concept and Hypotheses

Model Structure

Kumbhakar and Bhaumik (2010) apply stochastic frontier method in a cross-sectional framework to decompose output growth into input, technological and efficiency effects. This method is utilized to build a trade growth decomposition framework using stochastic frontier gravity models as follows:

Consider two *estimated* stochastic frontier 'inverse' gravity models for world trade for periods 1 and 2:

$$\text{Ln}Y_{ij}^1 = \alpha^1 + \text{Ln}f^1\left(X_{ij}^1; \beta^1\right) + V_{ij}^1 - U_{ij}^1, \qquad i.j = 1, \ldots, n. \qquad (1.1)$$

$$\text{Ln}Y_{ij}^2 = \alpha^2 + \text{Ln}f^2\left(X_{ij}^2; \beta^2\right) + V_{ij}^2 - U_{ij}^2, \qquad i,j = 1, \ldots, n \qquad (1.2)$$

where $\text{Ln}f^1\left(X_{ij}^1; \beta^1\right) = \beta^1 \text{Ln}X_{ij}^1$ and so on.

Taking the difference of the above equations and using $\text{Ln}f^1\left(X_{ij}^1; \beta^1\right) = \beta^1 \text{Ln}X_{ij}^1$ and so on, one gets

$$\text{Ln}Y_{ij}^2 - \text{Ln}Y_{ij}^1 = \beta^2\left(\text{Ln}X_{ij}^2 - \text{Ln}X_{ij}^1\right) + \left[(\alpha^2 - \alpha^1) + (\beta^2 - \beta^1)\text{Ln}X_{ij}^1\right]$$
$$+ \left(V_{ij}^2 - V_{ij}^1\right) - \left(U_{ij}^2 - U_{ij}^1\right), \qquad i,j$$
$$= 1, \ldots, n \qquad (1.3)$$

Taking the mean of the above equation, one gets

$$\left(\overline{\text{Ln}Y_{ij}^2} - \overline{\text{Ln}Y_{ij}^1}\right) = \beta^2\left(\overline{\text{Ln}X_{ij}^2} - \overline{\text{Ln}X_{ij}^1}\right) + \left[(\alpha^2 - \alpha^1) + (\beta^2 - \beta^1)\overline{\text{Ln}X_{ij}^1}\right]$$
$$- \left(\overline{U_{ij}^2} - \overline{U_{ij}^1}\right), \qquad i,j$$
$$= 1, \ldots, n \qquad (1.4)$$

where the bar denotes the sample mean of the respective variable. The third bracketed term of Eq. (1.3) vanishes in Eq. (1.4) as V_{ij} is distributed $N(0, \sigma_v^2)$.

The first three bracketed terms on the right-hand side of Eq. (1.4) (and the first, second and fourth term of Eq. (1.3)) correspond to the notions of 'input effect', 'technological effect' and 'efficiency effect' developed in Kumbhakar and Bhaumik (2010). The third term in Eq. (1.3) is defined as 'random effect' to capture the role of random shocks on trade growth.

Interpretation of Model Terms (Eqs. (1.3) and (1.4))

The interpretation of the terms in Eq. (1.3) are derived from the literature (relevant references stated in brackets). They have similar meaning for Eq. (1.4), except that they explain growth of average trade. Random effect component vanishes in Eq. (1.4) as the random error term has a zero mean.

Input effect (Kumbhakar and Bhaumik 2010): *Contribution of change in inputs to trade growth.* Input effect is posited to be captured by a movement along the trade frontier or by exploitation of the curvature of the trade (export) frontier.

Technological effect (Kumbhakar and Bhaumik 2010; Berkowitz et al. 2006): *Contribution of change in export productivity to trade growth.* Technological effect in output growth decomposition derives its concept from production theory. However, in trade growth decomposition, it is posited to arise from both trade and production theory as the exporting decision is an offshoot of the production activity. Technological effect is defined to arise from two components:

Transaction effect: Increased export productivity caused by reduction in transaction costs of exporting firms. Reforms reduce transaction (trade) costs by reducing *fixed costs of exporting* such as those related to gathering information about demand conditions in foreign markets, searching for new partners, monitoring trade alliances, trade procedures and so on. This promotes trade by allowing existing firms to produce more of existing as well as new products to old and new markets. It also encourages new firms to enter export markets. This concept is related to 'intensive' and 'extensive' growth margins, which has its roots in the heterogeneous models of international trade (Melitz 2008).

Production effect: Increased export productivity caused by changes to production structures. Production effect is created through scale economies, learning-by-exporting skills, in-house technical innovation and adoption, intra-industry trade, promotion of sophisticated growth boosting products and so on.

No association is made between these two concepts and the two components of technological effect. As changing production structures takes time, reforms are likely to enhance export productivity through higher transaction effect than production effect in the short run.

Technological effect is posited to be captured by shift in the trade (export) frontier. An outward (inward) shift is purported to represent increased (decrease) export productivity.

Efficiency effect or catch-up effect (Kalirajan 2010; Kumbhakar and Bhaumik 2010): *Contribution of change in technical efficiency to trade growth.* Efficiency effect is posited to be a movement from a position within the export frontier towards the export frontier.

Random effect: Effect of random shocks on trade growth. Sources of such shocks could be financial crises, exchange rate fluctuations, socio-political and environmental issues and innovations.

Expected Pattern of Trade Dynamics

Trade growth dynamics is expected to follow similar trends as reported for output growth in UNIDO (2005).

In general, in the initial stages, trade growth occurs via enhanced resource utilization or higher input effect (due to trade reforms). However, corresponding to the growth literature, where this stage continues till dictated by the law of diminishing returns, no such analysis has been undertaken in the present study.

In the next stage, trade growth becomes dependent on increase in export productivity or technological effect.

Finally, as countries try to reach the trade frontier by improving their trade performance and trade technologies, the efficiency effect, which generally stays negative in the initial stages of growth, becomes positive.

The above pattern gets affected by both positive and negative random shocks existing in the global economic environment.

Hypotheses on Trade Growth Patterns of Developing and Developed Countries

Based on UNIDO (2005), which presents stylized facts on productivity decomposition for output growth, following hypotheses are proposed for trade growth.

First Hypothesis (H1)
Input effect is expected to be larger for developing countries than developed countries.

Explanation: Akin to output growth, trade is expected to be governed by input effect in developing countries. In addition, as developing countries have higher trade costs than developed countries, reforms are expected to add to input effect by releasing inputs blocked in the supply chain.

Second Hypothesis (H2)
Technological effect, on average, is expected to be larger for developed countries than developing countries, as the former are the innovators of technology.

However, a reverse trend, if found, is attributed to the following reasons: (i) Poor trade performance of developed countries as compared to the developing countries during 2001–2007 (WTO 2008), which is the period of analysis; (ii) Increased fragmentation of production and trade networks in technologically sophisticated goods (the embodiments of innovation). This leads to a situation where developed countries export semi-finished technologically intensive goods to developing countries, which in turn, re-export them in finished form to developed countries. This may impute a lower production effect to developed countries (Lall et al. 2005 and so on); (iii) Sampling considerations and aggregation issues: Countries like Singapore and Hong Kong, which are usually found to determine the trade frontier (Armstrong, Drysdale and Kalirajan 2008) are not included in the sample due to data constraints. Also, the data is at an aggregate level, masking technological differences across sectors.

Third Hypothesis (H3)

Efficiency effect is expected to be higher (or positive) for developed countries and lower (or even negative) for developing countries.

Technological progress in developing countries occurs by adoption of techniques (for domestic and export) that are new in their environment and at the beginning of the learning curve but mature in developed countries. Thus, the transfer of techniques to developing countries by the developed countries leads, *ipso facto*, to a regress in inefficiency.

In contrast, the attraction effect of technological innovation carried out by frontier countries is powerful in countries in the technological neighbourhood of the innovative segment, as they have similar infrastructure to undertake such activity. Hence efficiency effect for developed countries is expected to be positive.

Note*: A combination of negative technological effect and positive efficiency effect for developed countries possibly indicates presence of a large negative transaction effect in these countries. This is because a positive efficiency effect is likely to be the outcome of a strong production effect as these countries are the innovators of technology.*

Fourth Hypothesis (H4)

The random effect is expected, in general, to be higher for developed countries than for developing countries.

Developed countries have strong interlinkages with world trade and production networks that allows easier access to inputs, investment opportunities, credit, transport facilities and the like. However, a converse pattern, if found, is attributed to the global financial crisis and the poor trade and production performance of developed countries during 2001–2007.

Reforms Evaluation Framework: Concept and Hypotheses

Concept

Reforms act like inputs in accelerating the growth process. In this paper, reforms are represented by pillars of the Global Competitiveness Index (GCI) (Global Competitiveness Report (GCR) (World Economic Forum and Harvard University (2010, p. 8))))—basic requirements, efficiency enhancers and innovation and sophistication factors—which help in transition of factor driven economies (least developed countries) to innovation driven economies (advanced economies). A low level of development is equated with a factor driven economy (in which 70% of export are primary commodities) where competitiveness is derived from certain basic requirements. Thereafter efficiency enhancers dominate before innovation and sophistication factors come to the fore (Table 1.1 gives details on these pillars).

Reforms influence trade by affecting trade growth components. The 'stage' of a reform area, measured by its depth and period of implementation, is posited to be directly related to the stage of trade growth dynamics. Thus, for instance, mature areas are expected to influence latter stages of trade growth in advanced countries.

Table 1.1 Coverage of various reform areas

GCR(x) (Reform area or index for measuring the area)	ICT (Source: WDI)	IMPCOU (Source: EFN)	PROP (Source: EFN)	NTB (Source: EFN)	IMEX (Source: EFN)	STABUS (Source: EFN)
Basic requirements						
Institutions		B	A			Burden of Government Regulations
Infrastructure	Telephone lines				Ports	
Macroeconomic stability						
Health and primary education						
Efficiency enhancers						
Higher education and training	Internet access in schools					
Goods market efficiency				Prevalence of trade barriers	Burden of customs procedures	Number of procedures and time required to start a business
Labour market efficiency						
Financial market sophistication						
Technological readiness	Except laws relating to ICT					
Market size						
Innovation and sophistication factors						
Business sophistication	X					
Innovation	X					

Source: Author

Six reform areas are included in the paper: **ICT** (Information and Communication Technology Expenditure)**, IMEX** (Import and Export Costs)**, NTB** (Tariffs and non-tariff barriers)**, PROP** (Protection of property rights)**, IMPCOU** (Functioning of courts) and **STABUS** (Regulations for starting a business). Table 1.1 reports the correspondences of these areas with GCI.

The stage of a reform area is determined by worldwide trends, relation with GCI pillars (higher level pillars associated with higher level of development) and other factors. Trends in elasticities of frontier estimation between 2001 and 2007 (Appendix Tables 1.11 and 1.12) are not considered due to poor trade performance of developed countries in this period and other reasons like the inverse gravity methodology (dependent variable is international trade divided by intranational trade of both partners). Classification of these areas is explained below:

ICT_{ij}, *intermediate/matured area:* Increased usage by countries over time across the globe (ITU 2010) and usage amongst leaders of ongoing Industrial Revolution 4.0 (which is based on ICT)—Canada, Japan, Germany, Australia, Austria and Switzerland) (Clarke-Potter 2019).[1] ICT plays roles of '*infrastructure*', '*technological readiness*' and '*innovation* and *sophistication*' pillars of GCI, depending upon various stages of trade growth.

$IMEX_{ij}$ *and* NTB_{ij}, *intermediate/mature areas:* $IMEX_{ij}$ covers issues relating to border related trade facilitation, inland infrastructure and logistics services and has a profound impact on trade (Francois and Manchin 2007; UNESCAP 2009). Border related trade facilitation costs are in a comparable range across developing and developed countries (Duval and Utoktham 2009, 2011a) due to the implementation of worldwide reforms (Doing Business 2006, 2008, 2009, 2010, World Bank). However, work is required in the other two areas (India's logistics costs are amongst the highest in the world at around 13% of GDP that impose an annual loss of around $20 billion to its GDP (Banik 2014). Moreover, logistics are expected to play an important role in fostering regional cooperation (UNCTAD 2007b).

A: Property rights, including over financial assets, are poorly defined and not protected by law ($=1$) or are clearly defined and well protected by law ($=10$); B: The legal framework in your country for private businesses to settle disputes and challenge the legality of government actions and/or regulations is inefficient (min $= 1$) and subject to manipulation or is efficient and follows a clear neutral process (max $= 10$).

ICT: Correspondence with GCR established based on Global Trade Enabling Report (World Economic Forum 2008), which is like GCR. 'X' denotes the indirect coverage of these areas by ICT.

IMPCOU, PROP, NTB: The EFN values for these three variables (IMPCOU, PROP and NTB) are sourced from GCR.

---

[1]https://blockheadtechnologies.com/these-are-the-six-countries-leading-the-fourth-industrial-revolution/

IMEX, STABUS: These two variables have partial correspondences with GCR as they are part of Doing Business Report. The common areas between the EFN and GCR are indicated in Table 1.1.

NTB_{ij} captures the coverage of trade policy barriers-tariff and non-tariffs (NTB). Tariff liberalization is already extensive worldwide due to WTO, however, scope for more reduction has been identified (Duval and Utoktham 2011a, 2011b; Kowaleski and Dihel 2009). Moreover, reduction in NTBs is now the crucial component in international trade policy (UNESCAP 2009; Das 2012).

$IMEX_{ij}$ and NTB_{ij} are associated with *'infrastructure'* and *'goods market efficiency'* and *'goods market efficiency'*, respectively, in Table 1.1. They also indirectly impact the last stage pillar.

$IMPCOU_{ij}$, $PROP_{ij}$ and $STABUS_{ij}$ *(domestic business investment), indeterminate areas:* These variables are possibly associated with ongoing reforms, as many developed countries feature in bottom ranks. These variables are directly associated with *'institutions'* and *'goods market efficiency'* pillars (STABUS with both). However, they also indirectly impact the later stage pillar related to innovation and sophistication.

Hypotheses

Two more hypotheses are tested for examining the role of reforms in influencing trade growth dynamics.

Fifth Hypothesis (H5)

The stage of a reform area, in terms of years and coverage of implementation, is directly related to the stage of trade growth dynamics.

Examples: **ICT** is expected to influence early stages of trade growth in developing countries (as many of them still feature in lower ranks of this variable) and later stages of growth in developed countries. Further, reforms, in general, are expected to influence the later (earlier) stages of trade growth in developed (developing) countries.

Sixth Hypothesis (H6)

Random effect is expected to be higher for all reform areas with trade orientation ($IMEX_{ij}$, NTB_{ij}) than those aimed at building domestic capacity ($PROP_{ij}$, $IMPCOU_{ij}$, $STARBUS_{ij}$). It is also expected to be higher for developed countries as compared to developing countries.

1.3.2.2   Econometric (Frontier) Model and Descriptive Statistics of Key Variables

Frontier Model

The trade decomposition equations in Sect. 1.3.2.1 (Eqs. (1.3) and (1.4)) are obtained by taking the difference of two cross-sectional stochastic frontier inverse gravity models between 2001 and 2007.

Inverse gravity model does away with the multilateral resistance terms that simplifies estimation. However, a consequence of this model is that model parameters represent combined performance of both trade partners. Thus, the trade growth decomposition components represent combined performance of both trade partners. However, variations in trade performances of developed and developing countries do exist (Shankar 2015).

Following specification of stochastic frontier inverse gravity model (Eq. (1.1)) is adopted (the inverse gravity model does away with the multilateral resistance terms):

$$\mathrm{Ln} Y_{ij} = \mathrm{Ln}\left[\left(\frac{X_{ij}}{X_{ii}}\right) \times \left(\frac{X_{ji}}{X_{jj}}\right)\right]$$

$$= \mathrm{Const} + \beta 1 \mathrm{Ldist}_{ij} + \beta 2 \mathrm{Lang}_{ij} + \beta 3 \mathrm{Contig}_{ij} + \beta 4 \mathrm{FTA}_{ij}$$

$$+ \beta 5 \mathrm{ReformArea}_{ij} + \beta 6 \mathrm{LnDomt}_{ii} + \beta 7 \mathrm{LnDomt}_{jj} + V_{ij}$$

$$- U_{ij}, \quad i.j$$

$$= 1, \dots, n. \quad i \neq j. \tag{1.5}$$

Variables used in Eq. (1.5) are listed in Table 1.2.[2] Six forms of Eq. (1.5), corresponding to each of the six reform areas, are estimated for 2001 and 2007. Model results are subject to robustness checks based on Duval and Utoktham (2011a). Results of the frontier estimation are provided in Appendix Tables 1.11 and 1.12.

Variables and Descriptive Statistics

Table 1.2 shows the variables used in the frontier estimation (Eq. (1.5)) along with their references. Some important trends of the dependent variable, **Ltrade_{ij}** and other variables—**TradeGrowth_{ij}** and the six reform areas (bilateral trade pair values)—are discussed below. Correlations between dependent variable and independent variables are also reported. These will be used for explaining results of trade growth decomposition in Sect. 1.4.

1. **Ltrade_{ij}:** Mean increases from (−12.42) to (−11.74). (Dvd: (−9.77), (−9.44); Dvg. (−14.13), (−13.06)—Increase)

---

[2]FTAs (along with the year they came into force): APEC, APEC-China (2001), ASEAN, ASEAN-China (Goods-2005, Services-2007), Canada-Chile (1997), Canada-Israel (1997), Chile-China (2006), Chile-India (2007), Chile-Japan (2007), Chile-Mexico (1995), EU, EU-Chile (Goods-2003, Services-2005), EU-Israel (2000), EU-Mexico (2000), EU-Turkey (1996), SAFTA (2006), India-Sri Lanka (2001), Israel-Mexico (2000), Japan-Malaysia (2006), Japan-Mexico (2005), Japan-Thailand (2007), Korea-Chile (2004), MERCOSUR (1994), NAFTA (1993), Thailand-Australia (2005), Turkey-Israel (1997), US-Australia (2005), US-Chile (2004) and US-Israel (1985).

Table 1.2 Variable definition

Variable	Definition	Source	Purpose	Reference
1. $LDIST_{ij}(-)$	Ln(Distance)	CEPII	Transportation costs.	Armstrong et al. (2008), Armstrong and Drysdale (2010).
2. $CONTIG_{ij}(+)$	Dummy for contiguity.	CEPII	Transport and communication advantage.	Armstrong et al. (2008), Armstrong and Drysdale (2010).
3. $COMLANG_{ij}(+)$	Dummy for common language.	CEPII	Communication advantage.	Armstrong et al. (2008), Armstrong and Drysdale (2010).
4. $STABUS_{ij}(+)$	Log(Index of Govt. Reglns in Starting a Bus. of Exp*Imp)	EFN	Government's Business Start-up Regulations (Reglns).	Duval and Utoktham (2009, 2011a, 2011b).
5. $FTA_{ij}(+)$	Dummy for membership in Regional Trade Agreements	WTO	Foreign Policy.	Armstrong et al. (2008), Armstrong and Drysdale (2010)
6. $ICT_{ij}(+)$	Log(ICT expenditure as a ratio of GDP of Exp*Imp)	WDI	Information availability, automation of customs procedures, technological readiness.	Wilson et al. (2004) and Duval and Utoktham (2009, 2011a).
7. $PROP_{ij}(+)$	Log(Protection of property rights index of Exp*Imp)	EFN	Property rights protection.	Anderson and Marcouiller (2002) and Duval and Utoktham (2009, 2011a).
8. $IMPCOU_{ij}(+)$	Log(Index of improper courts of Exp*Imp)	EFN	Contract enforcement mechanism.	Anderson and Marcouiller (2002) and Duval and Utoktham (2009, 2011a).
9. $IMEX_{ij}(+)$	Log(Cost of export and import index of Exp*imp)	EFN	Import and Export Costs.	Duval and Utoktham (2011a, 2011b), Francois and Manchin (2007), UNESCAP (2009).
10. $NTB_{ij}(+)$	Log(Index of Tariffs and Non-Tariff Barrier of Exp*Imp)	EFN	Foreign policy.	UNESCAP (2009), Das (2012), Duval and Utoktham (2011a, 2011b) and Kowaleski and Dihel (2009).
11. $LDOMT_{ii}$ (+) $LDOMT_{jj}$	Log (EFN country score)	EFN	Domestic Trade costs.	Shankar (2015)

(continued)

Table 1.2 (continued)

Variable	Definition	Source	Purpose	Reference
12. LTRADE$_{ij}$	Log[(Bilateral exports/ internal trade) of Exp*Imp]	TRADE COST DATABASE	Internal trade adjusted bilateral exports.	Shankar (2015)

FTAs are listed as a footnote
Source: Author

    High (2007): Belgium, Netherlands, Malaysia and Austria (high trade to GDP ratio); Germany, China, US, Japan, France, UK and Canada (leading merchandize traders in 2007) (WTO 2008) and Vietnam (high trade/GDP ratio, high trade growth and amongst top merchandize 50 traders in 2007).
    Low (2007): Colombia and Bangladesh (low trade to GDP ratio); Philippines and Sri Lanka (least export growth amongst sample countries and a decline in trade/GDP ratio during 2000–2007); Romania-Philippines, Bangladesh and Chile (negligible trade (WITS, export share, 2007)).
    Similar pattern of Ltrade for 2001 (not reported).
2. **TradeGrowth$_{ij}$:** Mean value in the sample is 0.68. (Dvd: 0.33; Dvg: 1.08)
    High:
    Country pairs: Colombia-Bangladesh (max), Turkey, China, India; Vietnam-Argentina, Chile, Brazil, Mexico; Romania-Japan.
    Low:
    Country pairs: Philippines-Romania (min), Israel; Chile-Bangladesh; UK-Philippines; Korea-Sri-Lanka; Thailand-Romania; Sri-Lanka-Israel; UK-Indonesia; Philippines-Sri Lanka; UK-Chile.
    Countries (Sample average trade growth):
    High: Vietnam (highest), China, India, Argentina, Belgium, Bangladesh, Colombia, Turkey, Netherlands, Switzerland.
    Low: Philippines (lowest), UK, Israel, Sri Lanka, France, Indonesia, US, Sweden, Italy, Australia.
3. **Correlations**-Dependent and independent variables.

Variables	Full Sample		Developed Countries		Developing Countries	
	2001	2007	2001	2007	2001	2007
Reforms: ICT, Impcou, Prop, Ntb, Imex, Stabus	0.51, 0.45, 0.51, 0.46, 0.56, 0.39	0.27, 0.41 0.42, 0.28, 0.29, 0.25	−0.26, −0.07, 0.21, 0.28 0.43, −0.34	−0.13, −0.01, 0.07, 0.12, 0.14, 0.15	0.53, 0.31, 0.33, 0.31, 0.42, 0.54	0.29, 0.38, 0.30, 0.11, 0.13, −0.03
Gravity: Contig, Comlang, Ldist, FTA	0.33, 0.18, −0.57, 0.41	0.34, 0.15, −0.57, 0.40	0.58, 0.22 −0.81, 0.49	0.56, 0.24 −0.78, 0.43	0.28, 0.14, −0.57, 0.48	0.32, 0.12, −0.55, 0.49
Domestic Trade Costs: Exp and Imp EFN Scores	0.33, 0.32	0.28, 0.28	0.08, 0.04	0.01, −0.05	0.23, 0.24	0.18, 0.21

Table 1.4 Trade growth decomposition—developed countries (Figures in percentages)

Reform area	Input effect	Technological effect	Efficiency effect	Random effect
ICT_{ij}	−15.69	100.59	−34.20	49.30
$IMPCOU_{ij}$	−31.64	60.95	31.37	39.32
$PROP_{ij}$	126.58	−82.22	22.38	33.26
NTB_{ij}	112.40	−127.68	59.99	55.29
$IMEX_{ij}$	15.87	−2.49	35.12	51.51
$STABUS_{ij}$	−8.97	47.55	38.15	23.26
Average	33.09	−0.55	25.47	41.99
Average without $PROP_{ij}$	14.39	15.78	26.09	43.74
Average growth	0.326 (log points)			

Source: Author

Correlations report a decline in value from 2001 to 2007 for most variables. Increase: (i) Full sample: **Contig**; (ii) Developed countries: **ICT, IMPCOU, STABUS, Comlang** and **Ldist**.; (iii) Developing countries: **IMPCOU, Contig, Ldist** and **FTA**. Possible reasons for these observations could be the inverse gravity model methodology, where dependent variable is different from normal gravity equations, and an increase in negative shocks to world trade in this period (Shankar 2015). Such shocks (not reported) also show up in frontier results in this paper in Appendix Tables 1.11 and 1.12.

4. ICT_{ij}: Mean increases from 3.40 to 3.48. (Dvd: 3.66, 3.57—Decrease; Dvg: 3.19, 3.41—Increase).

Top 10 2001	Top 10 2007
Malaysia (best), Korea, South Africa, China, US, Vietnam, Switzerland, Canada, Netherlands and Japan.	Malaysia (best), South Africa, Korea, Bangladesh, Switzerland, US, Japan, Netherlands, Canada and China.
Bottom 10 2001	Bottom 10 2007
Bangladesh (worst), Sri Lanka, Indonesia, India, Colombia, Russia, Argentina, Turkey, Mexico and Chile.	Indonesia (worst), India, Russia, Turkey, Sri Lanka, Mexico, Colombia, Chile, Spain and Romania.

Key Changes
Top 10: Bangladesh moves from bottom 10 in 2001 to top 5 in 2007. Vietnam moves out of top 10 in 2007.
Bottom 10: Romania and Spain in bottom 10 in 2007. Argentina (with Bangladesh) not in bottom 10 in 2007.

Note: Dvd. and Dvg. stand for groups of developed and developing defined in Tables 1.4 and 1.5, respectively.

Table 1.5 Trade growth decomposition—developing countries (Figures in percentages)

Reform area	Input effect	Technological effect	Efficiency effect	Random effect
ICT_{ij}	98.01	52.27	−44.14	−6.14
$IMPCOU_{ij}$	53.15	49.62	0.99	−3.76
$PROP_{ij}$	213.60	−107.01	−4.70	−1.89
NTB_{ij}	94.82	12.54	2.08	−9.44
$IMEX_{ij}$	75.12	41.68	−5.58	−11.22
$STABUS_{ij}$	72.98	23.43	4.05	−0.46
Average	101.28	12.09	−7.88	−5.49
Average without $PROP_{ij}$	78.82	35.91	−8.52	−6.21
Average growth	1.075 (log points)			

Source: Author

5. **IMPCOU$_{ij}$:** Mean increases from 3.25 to 3.31. (Dvd.: 3.94, 3.83—Decrease; Dvg: 2.71, 2.90—Increase)

Top 10 2001 Australia, Israel, UK, Switzerland, Germany, Netherlands, US, Canada, Sweden and Austria.	Top 10 2007 Switzerland, Germany, Sweden, Austria, Netherlands, Australia, Canada, France, Japan and UK.
Bottom 10 2001 Argentina, Indonesia, Russia, Romania, Bangladesh, Turkey, Philippines, Mexico, Colombia and Vietnam.	Bottom 10 2007 Argentina, Bangladesh, Italy, Mexico, Russia, Philippines, Brazil, Romania, Turkey and Indonesia.

Key Changes
Top 10: Israel and US out of top 10 in 2007; Switzerland, Germany, Sweden move up in rankings in 2007; France and Japan in top 10 in 2007.
Bottom 10: Italy in bottom 10 in 2007; Colombia and Vietnam out of bottom 10 in 2007; Bangladesh and Mexico further down.

6. **PROP$_{ij}$:** Mean increases from 3.24 to 3.81. (Dvd.: 4.07, 4.23—Increase; Dvg: 2.58, 3.47—Increase)

Top 10 2001 US, UK, Netherlands, Austria, Australia, Switzerland, Sweden, Germany, Canada and Belgium.	Top 10 2007 Switzerland, Austria, Germany, Sweden, Canada, Australia, Netherlands, Japan, France and Belgium.
Bottom 10 2001 Bangladesh, Indonesia, Vietnam, Russia, Argentina, Romania, Philippines, Turkey, Mexico and India.	Bottom 10 2007 Argentina, Russia, Indonesia, Bangladesh, Philippines, Mexico, Romania, Turkey, Vietnam and Colombia.

(continued)

Key changes

Top 10: US and UK out of top 10 while France and Japan move here in 2007; Switzerland, Austria and Germany improve further in 2007.

Bottom 10: India out in 2007; Argentina and Russia slide back in rankings in 2007; Colombia joins in 2007; Vietnam improves its rank in 2007.

7. **NTB$_{ij}$:** Mean increases from 3.62 to 3.69. (Dvd.: 4.04, 3.91—Decrease; Dvg: 3.29, 3.51—Increase)

Top 10 2001	Top 10 2007
Chile, Netherlands, Sweden, Austria, Belgium, UK, Australia, Germany, Spain and US.	Sweden, Chile, Austria, Belgium, Netherlands, Australia, Israel, France, Germany and UK.
Bottom 10 2001	Bottom 10 2007
Vietnam, Romania, Russia, Philippines, Indonesia, Bangladesh, Turkey, Sri Lanka, Colombia and Japan.	Argentina, Russia, Colombia, Vietnam, Brazil, Thailand, Sri Lanka, Philippines, Bangladesh and Switzerland.

Key changes

Top 10: Spain and US move out. Replaced by Israel and France in 2007.

Bottom 10: Romania, Indonesia, Turkey and Japan move out. Replaced by Argentina, Brazil, Thailand and Switzerland in 2007.

8. **IMEX$_{ij}$:** Mean decreases from 4.22 to 4.12. (Dvd.: 4.46, 4.34—Decrease; Dvg: 4.04, 3.95—Decrease)

Top 10 2001	Top 10 2007
UK, Belgium, Spain, Sweden, Italy, Australia, US, France, Germany and Switzerland.	US, Netherlands, Germany, Sweden, Austria, South Korea, Belgium, Switzerland, Canada and Spain.
Bottom 10 2001	Bottom 10 2007
Sri Lanka, Russia, Brazil, Argentina, India, Romania, Turkey, Bangladesh, Colombia and Philippines.	Russia, South Africa, Bangladesh, Vietnam, Indonesia, China, Chile, Sri Lanka, Mexico and Italy.

Key changes

Top 10: Italy from top 10 in 2001 to bottom 10 in 2007. UK, Italy, Australia and France replaced by Netherlands, Austria, South Korea and Canada in top rankings.

Bottom 10: Most of the countries in 2007 replaced over those in 2001 except Sri Lanka, Russia and Bangladesh.

9. **STABUS$_{ij}$:** Mean increases from 3.23 to 4.37. (Dvd.: 3.45, 4.47—Increase; Dvg: 3.06, 4.28—Increase)

Top 10 2001	Top 10 2007
US, UK, Canada, Australia, Malaysia, Israel, Thailand, Switzerland, Sri Lanka and Netherlands.	Australia, Canada, US, France, Belgium, Romania, Turkey, UK, Italy and Netherlands.
Bottom 10 2001	Bottom 10 2007
Romania, Argentina, Mexico, Colombia, France,	Indonesia, Brazil, Bangladesh, Philippines,

(continued)

Russia, Bangladesh, Belgium, Italy and Philippines.	China, Vietnam, Spain, India, Colombia and Sri Lanka.

Key changes
Top 10: Malaysia, Israel, Thailand, Switzerland and Sri Lanka replaced by France, Belgium, Romania, Turkey and Italy in 2007.
Bottom 10: Romania, France, Belgium and Italy move away to top 10 in 2007. Indonesia, Brazil, China, Vietnam, Spain, India and Sri Lanka move here in 2007.

1.4 Trade Decomposition and Reforms Analysis: Results

Equation (1.3) is calculated for each of the 1097 trade pairs for all the six models. Results for Eq. (1.4) are obtained by aggregating across four regions: (1) Full sample or world trade; (2) Trade between developed countries; (3) Trade between developing countries; (4) Trade between developing countries and all their trading partners.

1.4.1 Trade Growth Components

Trade growth patterns are presented in Tables 1.3, 1.4, 1.5, 1.6.

Trade decomposition modelling has been built around the concepts of growth accounting in this paper, as trade and output growth are related. A comparison with growth accounting estimates from a similar period would therefore provide a preliminary assessment of the methodology adopted in this paper.

APO (2012) reports contribution of total factor productivity growth (TFPG) to economic growth (goods and services) for a sample of 32 OECD and Asian countries for the period 2000–2010. Most of these countries are covered in this analysis. The report finds the TFPG share to be more than 40% on average for Asian countries and 50% or more for OECD countries. TFP in growth accounting is the sum technical

Table 1.3 Trade growth decomposition—full sample (Figures in percentages)

Reform area	Input effect	Technological effect	Efficiency effect
ICT_{ij}	86.42	61.67	−48.09
$IMPCOU_{ij}$	43.67	56.69	−0.36
$PROP_{ij}$	219.13	−112.57	−6.56
NTB_{ij}	110.68	−16.45	5.78
$IMEX_{ij}$	72.83	32.23	−5.06
$STABUS_{ij}$	65.55	33.13	1.32
Average	99.71	9.11	−8.83
Average without $PROP_{ij}$	75.83	33.45	−9.28
Average growth	0.682 (log points)		

Source: Author

Table 1.6 Trade growth decomposition: developing countries and all partners (Figures in percentages)

Reform area	Input effect	Technological effect	Efficiency effect	Random effect
ICT$_{ij}$	96.66	56.59	−47.81	−5.44
IMPCOU$_{ij}$	52.23	53.65	−1.85	−4.03
PROP$_{ij}$	223.53	−112.84	−7.71	−2.98
NTB$_{ij}$	105.54	0.43	1.14	−7.12
IMEX$_{ij}$	77.69	37.60	−7.78	−7.51
STABUS$_{ij}$	73.30	28.83	−0.11	−2.02
Average	104.83	10.71	−10.69	−4.85
Average without PROP$_{ij}$	81.09	35.42	−11.28	−5.22
Average Growth	0.846 (log points)			

Source: Author

progress, scale efficiency change, allocative efficiency change and technical efficiency change (Kim and Saravanakumar 2012). TFP is the sum of technological and efficiency effects in this paper.

The sums of technological and efficiency effects for developed and developing countries (for goods only) in Tables 1.4 and 1.6 (Average excluding **PROP$_{ij}$**) come to about 40% and 26%, respectively. Accounting for sampling and methodological differences, these estimates probably provide preliminary support to the methodology adopted in the paper. The patterns of trade growth components, derived from UNIDO (2005) for output growth, also conform to hypotheses outlined in Sect. 1.3.2.1 and are discussed below.

1.4.1.1 Overall Trade Growth (Log Points)

Highest average trade growth for Developing countries (1.075, Table 1.5) followed for Developing-All (0.846, Table 1.6), Full sample (0.682, Table 1.3) and Developed countries (0.326, Table 1.4). India: 1.464, China: 1.982. (Country pairs: Min: Romania-Philippines (−4.05), Max: Colombia-Bangladesh (8.90)).

This conforms to actual trade growth patterns (in percent) in the literature during 2000–2007 (WTO 2008, Table I.2, p. 7) (World—5.5, North Americas—4, Europe—4, Latin America and Asia—9, India and China—13 and 22.5).

It is also consistent with Besedes and Prusa (2007). Using the concepts of intensive and extensive margins, the authors find the highest gains in extensive margins for East Asia followed for Africa, India and Central and South American countries, respectively. US and EU register small gains. The authors propose that developed countries need to increase their trade potential by reorganizing their trade and production structures to keep up their trade potential vis-à-vis developing countries (where trade potential is still at an evolutionary stage and high).

1.4.1.2 Trade Growth Components as a Percentage of Average Trade Growth

Input effect. Highest for Developing-All (81.09, Table 1.6) followed for Developing (78.82, Table 1.5), Full sample (75.83, Table 1.3) and Developed countries (14.39, Table 1.4), respectively.

The trend supports Hypothesis **H1** that growth takes place by using inputs in the initial stages. Further, developing countries have substantial inputs blocked in the supply chain due to trade costs. Reforms, which release such inputs, also add to the input effect in developing countries.

Technological effect. Highest for Developing countries (35.91, Table 1.5) and Developing-All (35.42, Table 1.6), Full sample (33.45, Table 1.3) and Developed countries (15.78, Table 1.4), respectively.

The trend is contrary to Hypothesis **H2**. Sampling issues, level of aggregation over goods, presence of Asian countries in globalized production networks (Lall et al. 2005) and poor trade and production performance of developed countries vis-à-vis developing countries during 2000–2007 are provided as possible causes.

It also possibly confirms large negative transaction effect for developed countries due to falling market shares (WTO 2008) and low extensive and intensive margins (Besedes and Prusa 2007) in this period.

Efficiency effect. Highest for Developed Countries(26.09, Table 1.4). After that followed by Developing Countries (−8.52, Table 1.5), Full sample (−9.28, Table 1.3), and Developing-All group (−11.28, Table 1.6) respectively.

These observations support Hypothesis **H3**. This probably indicates that developed countries, being the innovators of technology, have strong production effect, which in turn gives rise to a positive and a higher magnitude of efficiency effect as compared to developing countries.

However, due to falling of trade potential in developed countries (Besedes and Prusa 2007) and the emergence of multipolar world (Lin 2011) developing countries also seem to be catching up. For instance, India and China have positive values.

Random effect. Highest for Developed countries (43.74, Table 1.4) followed for Developing-All (−5.22, Table 1.6) and Developing countries (−6.21, Table 1.5), respectively.

Random effect component supports Hypothesis **H4**. Thus, random factors, captured via interlinkages with world trade, investment and production networks promoted trade growth of developed countries. Developing countries suffered negative shocks, in the form of the Global Financial Crisis that had set in by 2008, depreciation of the US Dollar against major currencies during this period (UNCTAD Trade Development Report 2008) and other factors. This retarded their exports and hence trade growth.

The next section presents country level analysis for four reform areas—**ICT, IMPCOU, NTB** and **STABUS** (the other two not reported for space issues) through Tables 1.7, 1.8, 1.9, 1.10. This analysis is based on magnitudes (not percentages) as many trade pairs have negative growth. Also, for ease of reporting, these tables

Table 1.7 ICT—Trade growth decomposition (Figures in numbers (percentages in square brackets))

Input effect	Technological effect
Developed (−0.05) [−16]	*Developed (0.33) [101]*
Max: Fra-Jpn (0.55), Aut; Aut-Jpn; Fra-Che, Deu (0.33)	Max: Aut-Deu (0.92); Fra-Ita, Esp, Bel; Ita-Aut (0.83)
Min: UK-Swe (−0.35), Bel; Bel-Swe; US-UK, Swe (−0.33)	Min: Che-Nld (−0.25), UK, Swe, Esp, Bel (−0.08)
Developing-All (0.82) [97]	*Developing-All (0.48) [57]*
Bgd-Lka (4.33), Rom, Rus, Ind, Col, Idn, Zaf, Tur, Mex, Chl, Phl (3.38)	Bgd-Ind (1.38); Rus-Chn; Bra-Arg; Rus-Idn; Bgd-Lka; Idn-Mex; Chn-Vnm; Rus-Mex; Idn-Mys; Mex-US (0.98)
Vnm-UK (−0.37), Swe, Bel, US, Esp, Can , Aus, Nld, Bra, Mys (−0.22)	Mys (0.02), Kor-Che; Mys-UK; Zaf-Che; Mys-Nld; Kor-UK, Nld; Mys-Zaf; Mys, Kor (0.10)-Swe.
Efficiency effect	**Random effect**
Developed (−0.11) [−34]	*Developed (0.16) [49]*
Che-Can (1.17), Aus, Bel; Can-Nld; Che-Nld (0.60)	Bel-US (1.63), Aus, Can, Jpn, Swe (1.11)
Isr-Swe (−0.92); Fra-Isr, UK, Ita, Esp (−0.71)	Fra-Esp (−0.51), Ita, Isr; Isr-Swe; Fra-Deu (−0.28)
Developing-All (−0.41) [−48]	*Developing-All (−0.05) [−5]*
Col-Tur (3.54), Bgd; Vnm-Bra, Chl, Mex; Arg-Che; Vnm-Col, Tur; Can; Chn-Col (1.56).	Chn-Bel (2.13); Vnm-Mys, Arg, Bel; Chn-Col, Arg; Nld-Vnm, Chn; Chn-Bra; Vnm-US (1.64)
Chl-Bgd (−4.90); Rom-Phl; Bgd-Phl, Lka, Tha, Aus; Kor-Lka; Rom-Tha; Phl-Lka, Isr (−2.54)	Rus-Ind (−1.85), Lka; Bgd-Fra, Nld, Chl, Ita; Lka-Isr; Bgd-US; Lka-UK; Rom-Phl (−1.50)

Source: Author

record maximum values of a trade pair for each component when the difference between them is insignificant (e.g. max of **Bgd-Lka** and **Lka-Bgd** in Table 1.7).

1.4.2 Reforms Implementation

1.4.2.1 Country and Regional Patterns

ICT_{ij}

Input effect: **Maximum**: Bgd-Lka (4.33); **Minimum**: UK-Vnm (−0.37)

Bangladesh posted the highest increases of 6.1 (316 %) (Sri Lanka was second at 2.2 (90%)) for ICT variable during 2001–2007 and moved from bottom 10 in 2001 to top 5 in 2007. Vietnam posted the greatest decrease of −1.8 (24%). ICT possibly reflects the role of **infrastructure pillar** in fostering trade in Bangladesh.

Region: Developing countries score more than developed countries (percentage).
Technological effect: **Maximum**: Bgd-Ind (1.38); **Minimum**: Che-Nld (−0.25).

Table 1.8 IMPCOU—Trade growth decomposition (Figures in numbers (percentages in square brackets))

Input effect	Technological effect
Developed (−0.10) [−32]	*Developed (0.20) [61]*
Jpn-Fra (1.07), Aut, Esp; Fra-Aut, Esp (0.69)	Isr-Aus (1.03); Deu-Aut; Isr-Can, Swe, US (0.73)
Isr-Ita (−1.32), US; Ita-US; UK-Isr, Ita (−0.92)	UK-Che (−0.35), Bel, Nld, Ita; Nld-Che (−0.26)
Developing-All (0.44) [52]	*Developing-All (0.45) [54]*
Chl-Fra (2.37); Rom-Idn; Chl-Aut, Esp; Tur-Idn; Chl-Swe, Ind, Deu; Rus-Idn; Chl-Nld (1.76)	Chn-Ind (1.51), Rus, Vnm; Bra-Col; Ind-Isr; Chn-Mys, Col, Isr, Bra, Rom (1.18)
Lka (−1.10), Bra-Isr; Lka, Bra-Ita; Lka, Bra -US; Bra-US; Zaf-Isr; Lka-UK; Chn-Isr (−0.69)	Arg-Phl (−0.83), US, Can, Che, UK, Ita, Bel, Nld, Idn, Jpn (−0.55)
Efficiency effect	**Random effect**
Developed (0.10) [31]	*Developed (0.13) [39]*
Che-Can (1.07), Aus; Nld-Can; Che-UK, Bel (0.61).	Bel-US (1.85), Ita, Isr, Can, Aus (1.23)
Jpn-Swe (−0.64); Fra- Esp, Che, Jpn, Can (−0.50)	Jpn-Swe (−0.76); Fra-Jpn, Esp; Swe-Isr; Fra-Che (−0.60)
Developing-All (−0.02) [−2]	*Developing-All (−0.03) [−4]*
Col-Bgd (5.65), Tur, Ind; Vnm-Chl, Mex; Arg-Che; Bgd-Ind, Lka; Bra-Vnm; Rom-Jpn (1.32)	Arg-Vnm (2.29), Chn; Col-Chn; Vnm-US; Chn, Arg-Bel; Arg-Rus, Che; Bgd-Col; Rus-Arg (1.62)
Rom-Phl (−3.36), Tha, Idn; Chl-Bgd, Rom; Phl-Isr; Chl-UK; Idn-Aut, Col; Rom-Vnm (−1.34)	Rom-Phl (−2.15); Fra-Idn; Rom-Tha; Rus-Ind, Mys; Phl-Isr; Idn-Swe; Chl-Fra; Idn-Kor, Esp (−1.49).

Source: Author

Bangladesh's merchandize trade with India increased nearly 2.5 times between 2000–2001 and 2006–2007 from $1 to 2.5 billion, with trade being tilted in favour of India (Bangladesh's trade deficit with India increased from $1 to 2 billion). However, exports from Bangladesh to India nearly doubled between 2004–2005 and 2006–2007. Its import-export ratio declined from 20 in 2001–02 to 8 in 2006–07.[3] ICT reforms in Bangladesh, which helped in increasing jobs and productivity, are likely to have played some role here (UNCTAD (2007a)).

Second highest-Chn-Rus (1.28): China-Russia bilateral trade increased due to sanctions imposed on Russia's exports by European Union post the Crimean war in 2014 and China's growing energy needs, which were met by Russia. Share of Chinese imports into Russia increased from less than 5% in 2000 to around 15% in 2007 and China became Russia's second largest importer in 2007 (WITS Trade Summary 2001 and 2007). In addition, Chinese exports to Russia began to shift from labour

---

[3]https://www.financialexpress.com/archive/india-bangladesh-keen-on-joint-ventures-across-sec tors/350826/

Table 1.9 NTB—Trade growth decomposition (Figures in numbers (percentages in square brackets))

Input effect	Technological effect
Developed (0.37) [112]	*Developed (−0.42) [−128]*
Fra-Aut (1.15), Esp, Jpn, Che; Aut-Esp (0.96)	Che-Jpn (0.68), Ita; US-Can; Che-Fra, Deu (0.45)
Bel-Nld (−0.20), UK, US; Nld-UK, US (−0.17)	Swe-Isr (−1.22), Aut; Isr-Aut; Swe-Bel; Isr-Esp (−1.14)
Developing-All (0.89) [106]	*Developing-All (0.00) [0]*
Rom-Rus (3.26), Tur, Chn; Chl-Fra; Rus-Tur; Chl-Aut; Rom-Fra; Chl-Esp; Rus-Chn; Rom-Chl (2.45)	Phl-Vnm (1.40), Arg, Jpn, Rom, Lka, Bgd, Ind, Idn, Che, US (1.06)
Arg (−0.45), Lka-Phl; Arg-Lka; Phl, Arg-Bel; Phl, Arg-Nld; Phl, Arg-UK; Phl-US (−0.30)	Chn-Chl (−1.14), Isr, Swe, Aut; Chl-Isr-Swe; Chn-Esp, Bel; Chl-Aut; Chn-Aus (−0.93)
Efficiency effect	**Random effect**
Developed (0.20) [60]	*Developed (0.18) [55]*
Aut-Swe (0.99), Isr, Nld; Nld-Deu; Can-Che (0.73)	Bel-Isr (2.07), Swe, US, Aus, Ita (1.65)
Fra-Che (−0.59), Jpn; Jpn-Swe; Fra-Esp, Can (−0.29)	Fra-Che (−0.90), Jpn, Esp; Jpn-Swe; Fra-Can (−0.53)
Developing-All (−0.01) [1]	*Developing-All (−0.06) [−7]*
Col-Bgd (6.00), Tur, Ind; Chl-Vnm; Ind-Bgd; Vnm-Col; Lka-Bgd; Arg-Aut, Che; Mex-Vnm (1.37)	Chn-Col (2.62), Bel, Arg; Arg-Vnm; Chn-Nld, Zaf; Col-Bgd; Chn-Chl; Arg, Lka-Bel (1.72)
Rom-Phl (−3.70), Tha; Phl-Isr; Rom-Chl; Rus-Phl; Rom-Vnm, Idn, Isr; Chl-UK, Bgd (−1.18)	Rom-Phl (−3.06), Tha; Phl-Isr; Rus-Rom, Ind; Phl-UK; Chl-Bgd; Rus-Mys; Rom-Vnm, Chl (−1.75)

Source: Author

intensive to high technology level goods during 2001–2007 (Garcia-Herrero and Xu 2016, 2019).

These observations possibly reflect the role of ICT as both **infrastructure** and **technological readiness** pillars in fostering trade. Netherlands and Switzerland, being at the top 10 in both the years, possibly reflect low unrealized gains, amongst other factors.

Region: Developed countries score more than developing countries (percentage). **ICT** probably captures the role of technological readiness and to some extent 'business sophistication and innovation pillars' of GCI in developed countries in this period both through general impact (Spiezia 2011) and through trade in network products (Veeramani and Dhir (2019b)). The latter role of **ICT** is also reflected in ongoing fourth industrial revolution in these countries (Clarke-Potter 2019).

Efficiency effect: **Maximum**: Col-Tur (3.54); **Minimum**: Chl-Bgd (−4.89)

Bangladesh moved in top 5 in 2007, however, Chile, Colombia and Turkey were in bottom 10 in both years. However, World Bank's Doing Business (2013) records some changes in ICT reform area for Colombia- online submission of documents for registration of business in 2005 and introduction of electronic payment system for

Table 1.10 STABUS—Trade growth decomposition (Figures in numbers (percentages in square brackets))

Input effect	Technological effect
Developed (−0.03) [−9]	*Developed (0.16) [48]*
Fra-Aut (0.65), Jpn, Aus, Isr, Esp (0.51)	Fra-Bel (1.56), Ita, Esp, Jpn; Jpn-Bel (1.05)
Bel- Nld (−0.62), UK, Ita, US, Can (−0.51)	UK-Nld (−0.71); Isr-UK, Swe, Che, US (−0.63)
Developing-All (0.62) [73]	*Developing-All (0.24) [29]*
Rom-Rus (2.89), Tur, Idn, Chn; Rus-Tur; Rom-Vnm, Mys; Chl-Fra; Rom-Chl, Fra (2.04)	Arg-Mex (2.50), Rom, Fra, Bel, Col, Esp; Mex-Fra; Arg-Chl; Rom-Mex; Arg-Ita (1.82)
Arg-Bel (−1.04), Nld, UK, Italy, US, Lka, Can, Phl, Che, Swe (−0.69)	Mys-Lka (−1.27), Vnm; Tha-Idn, Lka; Mys-Idn; Tha-Isr, Mys, Vnm; Mys-Aus; Tur-Isr (−1.02)
Efficiency effect	**Random effect**
Developed (0.12) [38]	*Developed (0.08) [23]*
Che-Can (1.30), Aus, UK; Nld-Can, UK (0.81)	Bel-US (1.69), Isr, Can; Nld-US; Bel-Aus (1.22)
Fra-Esp (−0.76), Ita, Aut, Jpn, Che (−0.52)	Fra-Esp (−1.19), Jpn, Ita, Aut, Che (−0.82)
Developing-All (−0.00) [0]	*Developing-All (−0.02) [−2]*
Col-Bgd (5.82), Tur; Lka-Bgd; Col-Vnm, Ind; Bgd-Ind; Vnm-Chl, Can, Bra; Chn-Bgd (1.35)	Mys-Vnm (2.68); Col-Chn; Vnm-US, Arg, Nld; Zaf-Chn; Bra-Vnm; Chn-Nld; Tha-Vnm; Chn-Bel (1.62)
Rom-Phl (−3.79), Chl, Tha; Chl-Bgd; Rom-Col, Idn; Phl-Isr; Chl-UK; Rom-Isr, Vnm (−1.31)	Rom-Phl (−3.05), Tha, Fra; Chl-Fra; Rom-Ita, Chl; Chl-Bgd; Rus-Rom, Ind; Rom-Bra (−1.80)

Source: Author

tax compliance in 2002, for instance. Moreover, trade efficiency is likely to benefit from improvement in EFN country scores. Finally, growth values of **Col-Tur** pair (second highest) and **Chl-Bgd** (amongst the least) probably add to explanation.

Region: Developed countries score more than developing countries (percentage).

Random effect: **Maximum**: Bel-Chn (2.15); **Minimum**: Rus-Ind (−1.85)

China was in top 10 ICT rankings in both 2001 and 2007 and became the second largest importer of ICT goods in 2006 after US. It was the largest exporter of ICT goods in 2005 (UNCTAD 2007a). Belgium has excellent network infrastructure (UNCTAD (2007a)) and ICT sector accounted for sixth of GDP growth between 1997 and 2007.[4] Both Belgium and China featured amongst top exporters and importers of merchandize trade in 2007 and had high trade/gdp ratios in 2007. In general, countries with high trade growth, high trade/gdp shares score high in this component. Russia witnessed a decline in trade/gdp ratio after 2004 (below the world average) and had negative trade growth with India during 2001–2007.

Region: Developed countries score more than developing countries (percentage).

---

[4]https://www.business.belgium.be>ict

IMPCOU$_{ij}$

Input effect: **Maximum**: Fra-Chl (2.38); **Minimum**: Ita-Isr (-1.32).

France moved in top 10 sampled countries in 2007. Israel and Italy recorded largest decreases of -3.3 (-39%) and 1.6 (-35%), respectively.

Region: Developed countries score lesser than developing countries (percentage).

Technological effect: **Maximum**: Ind-Chn (1.51); **Minimum**: Arg-Phl (-0.83).

Chn-Ind (1.51) reflects efforts of increasing trade through bettering of political and institutional ties amongst other factors. China's bilateral trade with India increased from about $0.2 billion in 1990 to $5 billion in 2002 to $13.6 billion in 2004.[5] Similarly, Chn-Rus (1.45) reflects growing mutual relation with Russia, as discussed earlier under **ICT**, and, probably, growing trade within APEC region, as it accounted for 65% of China's total trade in 2006.[6] Argentina was the lowest rank holder amongst all sample countries in both years.

Region: Developed countries score more than developing countries (percentage).

Efficiency effect: **Maximum:** Bgd-Col (5.65).**: Minimum**: Rom-Phl (-3.36);

Colombia moves out of bottom 10 in 2007. This is confirmed by World Bank's Doing Business Report (2013), which finds that Colombia improved its performance on worldwide governance indicators pertaining to rule of law (which includes IMPCOU) between 2002 and 2010. Philippines features in bottom 10 in both years and had the least trade growth in the sample. Finally, **Col-Bgd** and **Rom-Phl** had the highest and least values of trade growth in the sample.

Region: Developed countries score higher than developing countries (percentage).

Random effect: **Maximum**: Arg-Vnm (2.29); **Minimum:** Rom-Phl (-2.15)

This possibly reflects greater trade integration (high trade/GDP ratio) and higher trade growth of Vietnam and poorer performance of Philippines (decline in trade/GDP ratio and trade growth in this period and also low rank under **IMPCOU**). Vietnam also moved out of bottom 10 in 2007. Finally, **Vnm-Arg** falls amongst high trade growth performers whereas **Rom-Phl** had the least trade growth.

Region: Overall, developed countries score higher than developing countries (percentage).

NTB$_{ij}$

The coefficient of **NTB$_{ij}$** variable decreases and becomes negative in 2007 while coefficients of domestic trade costs variables increase (Model 4, Tables 1.11 and 1.12). This trend is possibly explained in World Trade Report (2008), which states that trade liberalization becomes less important for trade when administrative barriers become more significant, as they act as a substitute for lower tariffs. This

---

[5]https://journals.openedition.org/chinaperspectives/2853#authors

[6]http://apec.org/Press/News-Releases/2007/0701_aus_iapchina

observation, along with decline in value of NTB_{ij} variable for developed countries, poor trade performance of developed countries during 2000–2007 (WTO 2008) could explain the results below.

Input effect: **Maximum:** Rom-Rus (3.26); **Minimum:** Arg-Phl (-0.45).

2007: Romania moves out of bottom 10 while Argentina falls to this category.

Romania (led by Indonesia) posts highest growth in this variable, whereas Argentina (followed by Switzerland) posts the least growth.

Region: Developed countries score *higher* than developing countries (percentage).

Technological effect: **Maximum:** Phl-Vnm (1.40); **Minimum:** Isr-Swe (-1.22).

Phl-Vnm has the third highest (though negative in magnitude and after **Vnm-Rom, Rus**) contributions of NTB_{ij} on total technological effect. Similarly, **Swe-Isr** has very low value of contributions of NTB_{ij} on total technological effect. Difference between magnitude of full technological effect for **Vnm-Phl** and **Swe-Isr,** in that order, is as follows:

$$NTB_{ij} : 3.17; Expscore : (-0.14); Impscore : (-0.38); Ldsit : (-0.03).$$

It is clear that **Vnm-Phl** scores lesser in all other three variables as compared to **Swe-Isr** and yet does better because of higher contribution of NTB_{ij} variable.

Region: Developed countries score *much lesser* than developing countries (percentage).

Efficiency effect: **Maximum:** Bgd-Col (6.00); **Minimum**: Rom-Phl (-3.70).

Col-Bgd and **Rom-Phl** had the highest and least values of trade growth in the sample. Moreover, as discussed above, due to increased relevance of domestic trade costs and other variables and decreased relevance of NTB_{ij} variable, efficiency effect is likely to be governed by other variables.

Region: Developed countries score more than developing countries (percentage).

Random effect: **Maximum:** Col-Chn (2.62); **Minimum:** Rom- Phl (-3.06).

Similar reasoning as for efficiency effect (least trade growth for **Rom-Phl**, high trade growth between **Col-Chn**) and increased value of **Efnscore** for China could be possible factors.

Region: Developed countries score higher than developing countries (percentage).

$STABUS_{ij}$

The variable $STABUS_{ij}$ depicts similar trend between 2001 and 2007 as found for NTB_{ij}. It becomes negative and insignificant during 2007 while coefficients of domestic trade costs and other variables increase in magnitude (Model 6, Tables 1.11 and 1.12). However, this variable increases in value for both developed and developing countries. These observations, along with poor trade performance of developed countries during 2000–2007 (WTO 2008) could explain the results below.

Input effect: **Maximum:** Rom-Rus (2.89); **Minimum:** Arg-Bel (−1.04).

Romania moves into top 10 in 2007 from bottom 10 in 2001. Top four countries with the highest increases and for this variable are Romania (7, 268%), Argentina (6.2, 233%), Fra (6.2, 178%) and Mexico (6, 200%).

Arg-Bel suffers from a negative value of domestic trade cost for Argentina in calculation of input effect (this component is positive and of a high magnitude for **Rom-Rus**).

Region: Developed countries score lower than developing countries (percentage).

Technological effect: **Maximum:** Mex-Arg (2.50); Minimum: Mys-Lka (−1.27).

Arg-Mex has the third highest contribution of $STABUS_{ij}$ (−3.99) on total technological effect (Highest for **Rom-Arg, Mex** at (−3.74) and (−3.95), respectively), whereas **Mys-Lka** low value of this contribution. (In percentage terms, Malaysia had the fifth least increase for this variable)

The full difference between **Arg-Mex** and **Mys-Lka** in technological effect calculation is as follows:

STABUS—3.32; Expscore—0.04; Impscore—0.01; Comlang—0.23; Ldist—0.18

It is clear that the main difference is due to the **STABUS** variable.

Region: Developed countries score higher than developing countries (percentage).

Efficiency effect: **Maximum:** Bgd-Col (5.82). **Minimum:** Rom-Phl (−3.79);

Similar reasoning as for NTB_{ij}.

Region: Developed countries score higher than developing countries (percentage).

Random effect: **Maximum:** Vnm-Mys (2.68); **Minimum:** Rom-Phl (−3.05).

Similar reasoning as in for NTB_{ij} (Vietnam reports high trade growth. Malaysia has a very high share of industry in value-added (Lin and Wang 2008), which probably requires good business-start up regulations- and that Malaysia was amongst the top 10 countries under this variable in 2001 possibly adds support to this assertion).

Region: Developed countries score more than for developing countries (percentage).

1.4.2.2 Summary

To sum up, findings at the regional level and country level lend some confirmation to the hypotheses **H5** and **H6** formulated for reform areas under Sect. 1.3.2.1:

(i) In general, frontier countries have lower input effects than factor driven economies.
(ii) ICT_{ij}: On average, frontier countries are found at top rankings.

Factor driven economies have higher input effect than frontier countries. However, aggregate technological effect is higher for frontier countries than factor driven economies. Efficiency effect is again higher for frontier countries.

So, model results support Hypothesis **H5**.

(iii) **IMEX$_{ij}$ and NTB$_{ij}$:** Here frontier countries do not depict a clear pattern. Many of them are out of top ranks in Global Competitiveness Report, GCR (World Economic Forum and Harvard University 2008).

For instance, **US, Switzerland, Germany** and so on are out of top 20 rankings in **NTB$_{ij}$**. Similarly, **UK, Italy, Australia** and **France** exited from top 10 sampled countries under **IMEX$_{ij}$**.

IMEX: On the aggregate, frontier countries have lower input effects than other stage countries. They also have higher technological effect and efficiency effects as compared to other stage countries. (Supports **H5**)

NTB: Frontier countries have higher input effect than factor driven economies. They also have much lower technological effect than them. However, they score more in efficiency component.

(iv) **IMPCOU$_{ij}$, PROP$_{ij}$** and **STABUS$_{ij}$**, indeterminate areas: Here, countries depict no clear pattern. Frontier countries like **Italy** feature in the bottom ten in reform areas like **IMPCOU$_{ij}$** and **Spain** features in the bottom ten under **STABUS$_{ij}$**. At the same time, transition countries like **Romania** and **Turkey** feature amongst the top ten under **STABUS$_{ij}$**. Model results, accordingly, reflect this heterogeneity.

STABUS$_{ij}$ and **IMPOUC$_{ij}$** depict a lower aggregate input effect as compared to other countries. Aggregate technological and efficiency effects are also higher. However, **STABUS$_{ij}$** reports a negative input effect for developed countries. **PROP$_{ij}$** reports a similar comparative pattern but has negative magnitudes of technological effect for all regions.

(v) The model can differentiate between reform areas with a trade or domestic orientation: Random effect is higher for **NTB$_{ij}$** and **IMEX$_{ij}$** as compared to **IMPCOU$_{ij}$, PROP$_{ij}$** and **STABUS$_{ij}$**. Similarly, countries that are favourably integrated in the global production and trade chains (high trade/GDP ratio and trade growth) have benefitted from positive random factors (Belgium, Vietnam, China and so on) while those in the reverse (Philippines, Sri Lanka and so on) have suffered. Aggregate random effect is also higher for developed countries as compared to developing countries. The model can, therefore, capture trade related shocks. This supports Hypothesis **H6**.

1.5   Conclusions

The results of the previous section indicate that the model outlined in this paper captures dynamics of trade growth and reforms at the aggregate level and country level. However, a more sophisticated modelling of trade dynamics and reforms evaluation is left as an area for future research.

The findings in this paper make the model a suitable quantitative tool for researches in trade and development. Few of these examples are discussed below.

The New Structural Economics (Lin 2010, 2011; Lin and Monga 2011) (NSE) deals with structural transformation and is closely related to the concepts developed in this paper. Further, UN-DESA (2015) cites NSE as one of the possible frameworks for promoting development by effecting structural transformation through trade. A sophisticated modelling of trade and output growth under NSE paradigm is left for further research.

The World Bank's Umbrella Facility for Trade Trust Fund (UF) was launched in 2017. As per World Bank (2018), it is expected to support four key areas of the World Bank's trade work in the coming six years: (i) trade competitiveness and diversification; (ii) trade facilitation and transport logistics; (iii) support for market access and international trade cooperation and (iv) managing shocks and promoting greater inclusion (e.g. trade and poverty; trade-gender linkages). The model developed in this paper can serve as a quantitative tool for assessing these areas.

Lastly, the Indian government recently outlined a $5 trillion vision for the Indian economy, to enable it to graduate out of its current low-income status. The Economic Survey 2019–2020 (Government of India 2020) recommends increasing exports of networked products (following China's example) to achieve this vision. Similarly, Forbes (2020) mentions India's biggest missed development opportunity to be its inability to participate in large-scale labour-intensive export manufacturing. The Flying Geese (FG) Model or East Asian Growth Model (related to NSE) explains the trade of labour-intensive and networked products and has been proposed as the model for guiding India's transition to a developed economy (Panagariya 2013; Srivastava 2016; Veeramani and Dhir 2019a; Forbes 2020). The framework developed in this paper can be used to project India's trade path to a developed economy, as guided by the FG model. However, as with NSE, more sophisticated modelling of structural transformation under Flying Geese Model is left as an area for future research.

Appendix 1

Table 1.11 Frontier estimation, world trace flows, 2001

	Model 1		Model 2		Model 3		Model 4		Model 5		Model 6	
	Coeff	SE	Coeff	SE	Coeff	SE	Coeff	SE	Coeff	SE	Coeff	SE
Const	−19.44	1.38	−17.74	1.72	−12.81	1.97	−19.60	1.66	−28.40	1.67	−19.32	1.56
$Ldist_{ij}$	−1.61	0.08	−1.46	0.09	−1.41	0.09	−1.50	0.09	−1.45	0.08	−1.61	0.08
$Comlang_{ij}$	0.00[a]	0.21	−0.16[a]	0.24	−0.07[a]	0.23	−0.15[a]	0.24	0.03[a]	0.23	−0.14[a]	0.23
$Contig_{ij}$	0.94	0.32	1.18	0.36	1.09	0.36	1.03	0.36	1.18	0.35	1.27	0.35
FTA_{ij}	1.01	0.14	1.51	0.16	1.63	0.16	1.50	0.16	1.15	0.16	1.22	0.15
ICT_{ij}	2.25	0.12										
$IMPCOU_{ij}$			0.79	0.14								
$PROP_{ij}$					1.33	0.18						
NTB_{ij}							1.19	0.30				
$IMEX_{ij}$									4.67	0.48		
$STABUS_{ij}$											1.68	0.18
$LDomt_{ii}$	4.03	0.46	4.56	0.61	2.67	0.71	4.67	0.68	2.80	0.62	4.58	0.53
$LDomt_{ij}$	3.89	0.46	4.44	0.61	2.54	0.71	4.57	0.68	2.67	0.62	4.43	0.53
Log-likelihood	−2278.81		−2406.99		−2394.98		−2414.19		−2378.08		−2382.30	
Lambda	1.75		1.57		1.55		1.47		1.45		1.54	
N	1097		1097		1097		1097		1097		1097	

Notes: Coeff is the model coefficient, while SE is the standard error; The log-likelihood test for Frontier Methodology is significant in all regressions
Source: Author calculations
[a]Implies that the variable is not significant

Appendix 2

Table 1.12 Frontier estimation, world trade flows, 2007

	Model 1		Model 2		Model 3		Model 4		Model 5		Model 6	
	Coeff	SE	Coeff	SE	Coeff	SE	Coeff	SE	Coeff	SE	Coeff	SE
Const	−17.56	2.39	−9.68	2.89	−10.74	2.74	−22.16	2.44	−22.88	2.48	−21.21	2.75
Ldist$_{ij}$	−1.51	0.09	−1.36	0.09	−1.35	0.09	−1.46	0.09	−1.41	0.09	−1.44	0.10
Comlang$_{ij}$	0.14[a]	0.24	0.12[a]	0.25	0.10[a]	0.25	0.09[a]	0.26	0.11[a]	0.26	0.09[a]	0.26
Contig$_{ij}$	1.36	0.37	1.59	0.39	1.50	0.38	1.55	0.40	1.61	0.40	1.61	0.40
FTA$_{ij}$	1.43	0.16	1.48	0.17	1.59	0.17	1.34	0.17	1.35	0.17	1.30	0.17
ICT$_{ij}$	2.06	0.20										
IMPCOU$_{ij}$			1.47	0.20								
PROP$_{ij}$					2.41	0.29						
NTB$_{ij}$							−0.92	0.40				
IMEX$_{ij}$									1.06	0.40		
STABUS$_{ij}$											−0.24[a]	0.65
LDomt$_{ii}$	3.50	0.79	1.74	0.97	0.86[a]	0.99	7.27	0.90	5.33	0.84	6.38	0.89
LDomt$_{jj}$	3.44	0.79	1.56[a]	0.97	0.71[a]	0.99	7.12	0.90	5.17	0.84	6.23	0.89
Log-likelihood	−2457.75		−2480.97		−2474.38		−2505.13		−2504.33		−2507.72	
Lambda	1.74		1.39		1.41		1.24		1.23		1.26	
N	1097		1097		1097		1097		1097		1097	

Notes: Coeff is the model coefficient, while SE is the standard error; The log-likelihood test for Frontier Methodology is significant in all regressions
Source: Author calculations
[a]Implies that the variable is not significant

References

Acharya, S. (2019). *Why neglect exports?* Business Standard, Retrieved from https://www.business-standard.com/article/opinion/why-neglect-exports-119121200067_1.html

Anderson, J., & Marcouiller, D. (2002). Insecurity and the pattern of trade: An empirical investigation. *Review of Economics and Statistics, 84*(2), 171–189.

APO. (2012). *APO productivity databook 2012, July.* Tokyo: APO.

Armstrong, S., & Drysdale, P. (2010). International and regional cooperation: Asia's role and responsibilities. *Asian Economic Policy Review, 5*(2), 157–173. Paper Prepared for Discussion at the Asian Economic Policy Review Conference, Tokyo.

Armstrong, S., Drysdale, P., & Kalirajan, K. (2008). Asian trade structures and trade potential: An initial analysis of South and East Asian Trade. EABER Working Paper, No 28. Retrieved September, 2009, from www.ncaer.org/downloads/Lectures/EABER-NCAER2008/s3p1.pdf

Banik, N. (2014). India-ASEAN free trade The untapped potential. CUTS International Briefing Paper No 3. Accessed on: January 20, 2021 from: https://www.nilanjanbanik.in/workingpaper/ASEAN_FTA_Paper.pdf

Berkowitz, D., Moenius, J., & Pistor, K. (2006). Trade, law and product complexity. *The Review of Economics and Statistics, 88*(2), 363–373.

Besedes, T., & Prusa, T. J. (2007). *The role of extensive and intensive margins and export growth. Working Paper No. 13628.* Cambridge, MA: National Bureau of Economic Research, Inc..

Clarke-Potter, K. (2019). These Are The Six Countries Leading The Fourth Industrial Revolution. Retrieved from: https://blockheadtechnologies.com/these-are-the-six-countries-leading-the-fourth-industrial-revolution/

Das, R. U. (2012). *Regional trade and integration: Analytical insights and policy options.* New York: Singapore, World Scientific. (Co-authored with Edirisuriya, P. and Swarup, A.).

Duval, Y., & Utoktham, C. (2009). *Behind the border trade facilitation in the Asia-Pacific: Costs of trade, credit information, contract enforcement and regulatory coherence.* Working Paper. No 67, Asia-Pacific Research and Training Network on Trade (ARTNeT), United Nation Economic and Social Commission for Asia-Pacific (UNESCAP), Bangkok.

Duval, Y., & Utoktham, C (2011a). *Trade facilitation in the Asia and Pacific: Which policies and measures affect trade costs the most?* Working Paper. No 94, Asia-Pacific Research and Training Network on Trade (ARTNeT), United Nation Economic and Social Commission for Asia-Pacific (UNESCAP), Bangkok.

Duval, Y., & Utoktham, C. (2011b). *Trade costs in the Asia and the Pacific: Improved and sectoral estimates.* Trade and Investment Division Staff Working Paper 05/11, Asia-Pacific Research and Training Network on Trade (ARTNeT), United Nation Economic and Social Commission for Asia-Pacific (UNESCAP), Bangkok.

Evenett, S. J., & Venables, A. J. (2002). *Export growth in developing countries: Market entry and bilateral flows.* University of Bern Working Paper, Mimeo.

Feenstra, R., & Rose, A. K. (1997). *Putting things in order: Patterns of trade dynamics and growth.* NBER Working Papers No. 5975, National Bureau of Economic Research, Cambridge, MA.

Forbes, N. (2020). *Growth matters* (p. 9). Business Standard.

Francois, J., & Manchin, M. (2007). *Institutions, infrastructure and trade.* Paper Retrieved from http://ssrn.com/abstract=964209.

Garcia-Herrero, A., & Xu, J. (2016). *The China–Russia trade relationship and its impact on Europe.* Bruegel Working Paper, No. 4. Retrieved from http://bruegel.org/wp-content/uploads/2016/07/WP-2016_04-180716.pdf

Garcia-Herrero, A., & Xu, J. (2019). How does China fare on the Russian market? Implications for the European Union. *Russian Journal of Economics, 5*, 385–399.

Hummels, D., & Klenow, P. J. (2005). The variety and quality of a nation's exports. *American Economic Review, 95*(3), 704–723.

International Telecommunication Union. (2010). *Measuring the information society: The ICT development index.* Place des Nations CH-1211, Geneva, Switzerland.

Jepma, C. J. (1986). *Extensions and application possibilities of the constant-market-shares analysis.* Groningen: Rijkusuniversiteit.

Kalirajan, K. (2010). Sources of variation in export flows over time: A suggested methodology of measurement. *International Journal of Business and Economics, 9*(2), 175–178.

Kalirajan, K., & Khan, I. U. (2011): The impact of trade costs on export growth: An empirical modelling. Foundation for Advanced Studies on International Development, Tokyo, Japan. Retrieved August, 2009, from http://www.crawford.anu.edu.au/acde/asarc/pdf/papers/2011/WP2011_07.pdf

Kim, S., & Saravanakumar, M. (2012). Economic reforms and total factor productivity growth in indian manufacturing industries. *Review of Development Economics, 16*(1), 152–166.

Kowaleski, P., & Dihel, N. (2009). *India's trade integration, realizing the potential.* OECD Trade Policy Working Paper No. 88, OECD Publishing.

Kumbhakar, S. C., & Bhaumik, S. K. (2010). Is the post-reform growth of the Indian manufacturing sector efficiency driven? Empirical evidence from plant-level data. *Journal of Asian Economics, 21*(2), 219–232.

Lall, S., Weiss, J., & Zhang, J. (2005). *The sophistication of exports: A new measure of product characteristics.* Tokyo: Asian Development Bank Institute, Discussion Paper No. 23. Retrieved from http://www.adbi.org.

Lin, J-Y. and Wang, Y. (2008). China's Integration with the world Development as a process of learning and industrial upgrading, Policy Research Working Paper No. 4799, Washington, World Bank, December.

Lin, J.-Y. (2010). *New structural economics: A framework for rethinking development.* Policy Research Working Paper No. 5197, Washington, World Bank, February.

Lin, J.-Y. (2011). *From flying geese to leading dragons: New opportunities and strategies for structural transformation in developing countries.* Policy Research working paper no. 5702, Washington, World Bank, June.

Lin, J.-Y., & Monga, C. (2011). *Growth identification and facilitation: The role of the state in the dynamics of structural change.* Policy Research working paper no. 5313, Washington, World Bank, May.

Melitz, M. (2008). International trade and heterogenous firms. in *New Palgrave dictionary of economics* (2nd ed.). Palgrave, Macmillan.

Ministry of Finance, Government of India. (2020). *Economic survey 2019–20.* Retrieved March, 4, 2020 from https://www.indiabudget.gov.in/economicsurvey/doc/echapter.pdf

Novy, D. (2009). Gravity redux: Measuring international trade costs with panel data. University of Warwick.

Novy, D. and Chen, N. (2009). International trade integration: A disaggregated approach. Retrieved from http://ssrn.com/abstract=1275688

Panagariya, A. (2013). *Indian economy: retrospect and prospect.* Canberra: Productivity Commission.

Roy, J. (2019). *Quick fixes won't solve the growth problem.* Business Standard, Retrieved from https://www.business-standard.com/article/opinion/quick-fixes-won-t-solve-growth-problem-119090800845_1.html.

Sala-i-Martin, X (Various issues). The Global Competitiveness Report. New York: Oxford University Press

Shankar, P. (2015). On the "frontier" estimation of the "inverse" gravity model: Insights and implications. *Indian Economic Journal, 63*(3), 362–384.

Spence, M. D., & Karingi, S. N. (2011). *Impact of TF mechanisms on export competitiveness in Africa.* Working Paper. No. 85, African Trade Policy Centre, United Nation Economic Commission for Africa.

Spiezia, V. (2011). Are ICT users more innovative? An analysis of ICT-enabled innovation in OECD firms. *OECD Journal: Economic Studies, 2011,* 1.

Srivastava, S. (2016). *The flying geese paradigm: "The Economics of Jugaad".* Retrieved from https://qrius.com/flying-geese-paradigm-economics-jugaad/amp/.

UNCTAD. (2007a). *Information economy report 2007–08. Science and technology for develop-ment: The new paradigm for ICT*. New York and Geneva: United Nations Publication. Sales No. E.07.II.D.13.

UNCTAD. (2007b). *Trade and development report 2007. Regional cooperation for development*. New York and Geneva: United Nations Publication. Sales No. E.07.II.D.11.

UNCTAD. (2008). *Trade and development report 2008. Commodity prices, capital flows and the financing of investment*. New York and Geneva: United Nations Publication. Sales No. E.08.II. D.21.

UN-DESA. (2015). *Workshop on productive capacity and the use of trade-related ISMs for LDC graduation*. Retrieved frm November, 3–5, frm https://www.un.org/development/desa/dpad/ 2015/workshop-on-productive-capacity-and-the-use-of-trade-related-isms-for-ldc-graduation/, 3–5 November 2015, Geneva.

UNESCAP. (2009). *Designing and implementation trade facilitation in Asia and the Pacific*. November 2009. Retrieved May, 2010, from http://aric.adb.org

UNIDO. (2005). Productivity in developing countries: Trends and policies, Vienna.

Veeramani, C., & Dhir, G. (2019a). *Reaping gains from global production sharing: Domestic value addition and job creation by Indian exports*, IGIDR Working Paper No WP-2019-024, Mumbai. Retrieved from http://www.igidr.ac.in/pdf/publication/WP-2019024.pdf

Veeramani, C., & Dhir, G. (2019b). *"Dynamics and Determinants of Fragmentation Trade: Asian Countries in Comparative and Long-term Perspective"* IGIDR Working Paper No WP-2019040, Mumbai. Retrieved from http://www.igidr.ac.in/working-paper-dynamics-determinantsfragmentation-trade-asian-countriescomparative-long-term-perspective/

World Bank. (2018). *Stronger open trade policies enable economic growth for all*. Results Briefs. April 3, 2018.

World Bank. (n.d.). *Doing business report*. Various Issues.

World Economic Forum and Harvard University (2010). *The global competitiveness report*. Geneva: World Economic Forum. World Economic Forum and Harvard University (2010). *The global competitiveness report*. Geneva: World Economic Forum.

World Economic Forum (2008). Global Trade Enabling Report 2008. Retrieved 20.01.2021 from: https://web.archive.org/web/20081206135156/http://www.weforum.org/pdf/GETR08/ GETR2008_FullReport.pdf

World Trade Organization. (2008). *World trade report*. Geneva: World Trade Organization.

World Bank. Doing Business (2013) Report. Various Issues

WTO. (2008). International trade statistics.

Chapter 2
An Empirical Analysis of Foreign Direct Investment (FDI) and Banking Sector Development (BSD) in West Africa

King David Kweku Botchway and Rajorshi Sen Gupta

2.1 Introduction

Policymakers in developing countries have increased their efforts to attract more FDI in recent years. Their interest is partly because of the relatively less volatile nature of FDI to other forms of capital flows, such as syndicated bank loans and equity flows. The high volatility of the other forms of capital flows to developing countries is an indication of the prevailing default risk, according to international investors. It reinforces the idea that developing countries view FDI as a critical source of long-term capital needed to break away from the low-level equilibrium trap that they face.

FDI and BSD are viewed as significant contributors to economic growth unilaterally or in unison. The former introduces new technology in the form of innovative processes and new capital goods, productivity, and competitiveness; the latter mobilizes savings for borrowers and enables efficient capital allocation. The innovative processes and modern capital introduced into host countries create spillover effects from the multinational companies to domestic firms. This is captured in the follower-leader hypothesis (FLH) by Barro and Sala-i-Martin (2003). The FLH suggests that domestic firms find it relatively cheaper to imitate new technologies than to invent. Recent reports from the United Nations Conference on Trade and Development infer that trends in announced Greenfield FDI projects in Africa have shifted from natural resource focused investments to manufacturing and the services sector (UNCTAD 2018). This means that value additions are created; employment increased which eventually increases economic growth.

The financial landscape in West Africa is mainly dominated by the banking sector (IMF 2016). The sector accounts for more than 60% of financial sector assets

K. D. K. Botchway · R. Sen Gupta (✉)
Department of Economics, BITS-Pilani K K Birla Goa Campus, Sancoale, Goa, India
e-mail: p20170010@goa.bits-pilani.ac.in; rajorshis@goa.bits-pilani.ac.in

according to the data available from the International Monetary Fund report, 2016, on financial developments in sub-Saharan Africa. As of 2014, stock exchanges and pension funds within the nonbank financial sector contributed 30% of total financial bank assets in West Africa. The French West African countries have a regional stock exchange serving all eight countries since 1998. The English West African countries have individual stock exchanges except for Gambia and Sierra Leon that have none.

There is a dearth of studies on the direct causal relationship between FDI and BSD in the context of West Africa. Previous studies mainly focused only on private credit as a proxy for financial development in West Africa. In this study, the ratio of liquid liabilities and total assets to GDP are examined alongside private credit to determine the nature of causality in West Africa. This study aims to provide an analysis of the existence and direction of the causal relationship between FDI and BSD using panel data from 1990 to 2016. This study will contribute to the FDI-BSD literature by finding answers to the question:

Does the increase in FDI inflows lead to the growth of financial systems in both French West Africa (henceforth FWA) and English West Africa (henceforth EWA)?

On the other hand, does an expansion in financial systems induce more FDI into both French and English West Africa? From the Granger causality analysis, the study finds a unidirectional relationship from BSD to FDI in both regions. The remaining of this paper is organized as follows: Sect. 2.2 provides a review of related literature, Sect. 2.3 discusses the data and method of analysis, and the empirical result in Sect. 2.4, and conclusion in Sect. 2.5.

2.2   Review of the Literature on FDI and BSD

This section aims to give an overview of theoretical and empirical evidence that explains the relationship between FDI and BSD. In general, the economic theory posits that FDI flows and BSD have a positive and significant relationship.

Bilir et al. (2019), Feinberg and Phillips (2004), using comprehensive U.S. micro-level data examined cross border greenfield investments by US multinational corporations (MNCs) and found that host countries with more significant capital market development do not pose growth constraints to affiliates of the US MNCs, whereas host countries with restrictions on FDI and underdeveloped financial markets constrained their expansion drive.

Desbordes and Wei (2017) using cross-country firm-level data on FDI investigated the effects of source and destination countries' financial development on Greenfield investments. The authors found that both source and destination financial development positively and significantly cause FDI inflows directly. The authors also observe that the host country's financial development indirectly promotes economic activities.

Chen et al. (2015) used a micro-level dataset of Chinese manufacturing firms to examine the link between regional financial development and foreign direct investment. The results show that a well-developed regional financial sector induces more

FDI inflows into the Chinese manufacturing sector. The study also found that local manufacturing firms in financially developed regions enjoy positive externalities from direct foreign investment.

Huang (2011) studied the causality between aggregate private investments and financial development using 43 developing countries from 1970 to 1998. By allowing for entity heterogeneity, the author found causality in both directions using GMM estimation. This means that financial development served as a boost to private investment and vice versa. Abimbola and Oludiran (2018) studied the significant determinants of FDI in the West African Economic and Monetary Union (WAEMU) for the period 1980–2010 using the panel cointegration approach. The finding from their study shows that there is a positive and significant relationship between FDI and financial development. Similarly, Anyanwu and Yameogo (2015); Anyanwu (2012) analyzed the factors that drive FDI into West Africa and Africa, respectively, using the least squares and generalized method of moment estimation methodology. The results showed a negative and significant relationship between FDI and financial development.

Soumaré and Tchana Tchana (2015) used cross-country data on 29 emerging markets to study FDI and financial market development relationship. The results showed that FDI and stock market variables are significant and positively impact each other. In the case of banking sector variables, the authors observed that FDI causes private credit and liquid liabilities.

Otchere et al. (2016) using both banking and stock market variables studied the direct causal relationship between foreign direct investment and financial market development in Africa over the period 1996–2009. Using the Granger non-causality test hypothesis, they find bidirectional causality by rejecting the null hypothesis of homogenous causality. This means that causality is heterogeneous among the countries chosen for the study.

Gebrehiwot et al. (2016) used a panel of eight African countries to study the FDI-financial development nexus. The authors found FDI and private credit to be positive and statistically significant using a 2SLS estimation procedure, whereas liquid liabilities statistically insignificant. The test for Granger causality revealed unidirectional causality from private credit to FDI but no causation in the case of liquid liabilities. Country-specific studies exploring the causal relationship between FDI and financial development in the West African context include Adam and Tweneboah (2009), OlugBenga and Grace (2015), Musa and Ibrahim (2014). These country-specific studies focused mainly on the relationship between stock market development and FDI, leaving out banking sector variables. The causal links between stock market variables and FDI were exempted in their study except for cointegration analysis.

2.3 Data and Methodology

Data on 12 countries from West Africa were collected for this study. There are eight countries in FWA: Benin, Burkina Faso, Senegal, Niger, Guinea, Ivory Coast, Mali, and Togo; four in EWA: Gambia, Ghana, Nigeria, and Sierra Leone. Data on the four variables from 1990 to 2016 are used. Descriptions of the variables are typically provided in Table 2.1. Following Alfaro et al. (2004), Okeyere et al. (2016), the below mentioned BSD variables are used. To analyze the relationship of growth of FDI and BSD in West Africa, the Holtz-Eakin et al. (1988) approach is used. In the panel data analysis literature, testing for the cross-sectional dependence is essential because it informs on the choice of panel unit root test to be applied. Granger causality analysis requires that the variables are stationary; hence panel unit root test is conducted on all the variables. Furthermore, the standard Wald test is also used to determine the direction of causality.

2.3.1 Cross-Sectional Dependence Test

The growing interdependence of countries in the last few decades (in the economic and financial front) has drawn the attention of researchers to relax the assumption of independence across individual time series in a panel setting. Dependence may take two forms: spatial or distance decaying dependence, where nearer individual cross-sectional units experience the most impact from a shock relative to entities that are farther away. This follows Tobler's First Law of Geography, "*Everything is related to everything else. But near things are more related than distant things.*" Pesaran and Tosetti (2011) describe this kind of dependence as weak form of cross-sectional dependence.

Table 2.1 Definition of variables

Variable	Definition	Source
G(CCA)	Growth of the ratio of commercial bank assets to the sum of commercial bank and central bank assets. Alternatively, the growth of the ratio of total bank assets.	The World Bank's Global Development Finance database
G (C/GDP)	Growth of the ratio of total private sector credit to GDP.	The World Bank's Global Development Finance database
G(FDI/ GDP)	Growth of the ratio of foreign direct investment to GDP.	World Development Indicators database
G (LL/GDP)	Growth of the ratio of liquid liabilities of the financial system to GDP.	The World Bank's Global Development Finance database

Note: The variables are defined following the World Development Indicators, published by the World Bank

The other form of dependence does not consider the distance of the individual units, but rather, the correlation among them is assumed to emanate from their exposure to the same cross-sectionally invariant common or global factors. For example, a boom or bust on a regional stock exchange or changes in global commodity (for example, oil) prices. Pesaran and Tosetti (2011) describe this kind of dependence as strong form of cross-sectional dependence. In the context of regional FDI growth, cross-sectional dependence can be introduced due to national policies aimed at attracting FDIs to their respective countries. Although these national policies may be common to all the countries, the effect is heterogenous due to country-specific characteristics. Hence this paper assumes a strong cross-sectional dependence of the individual time series variables; hence unit root test assumes a null hypothesis of cross-sectional independence using the common factor approach. The factor-augmented panel model is considered as follows:

$$y_{it} = \gamma_i^T z_{it} + \delta_i^T f_t + \epsilon_{it} \tag{2.1}$$

where y_{it} is the individual time series variable, $i = 1, \ldots, N$ is the cross-sectional index, and $t = 1, \ldots, T$. z_{it} is a vector of observed exogenous regressors and f_t is a vector of unobserved cross-sectionally invariant common factors. Pesaran (2007) proposes a test for cross-sectional dependence known as the Pesaran CD-test given by

$$CD = \sqrt{\frac{2T}{N(N-1)}} \left(\sum_{i=1}^{N-1} \sum_{j=i+1}^{N} \widehat{\rho}_{ij} \right) \tag{2.2}$$

under the null and alternative hypothesis as follows:

H_o: cross-sectional independence
H_1: cross-sectional dependence

2.3.2 Panel Unit Roots Tests

According to Baltagi (2008), it is prudent to examine the panel data for possible elimination of first-order integration to avoid spurious regression estimates. A regression equation of non-stationary series may give an appearance of a strong correlation even though the covariates may not have strong explanatory power or zero explanatory power. The fundamental test to check for unit root is the Augmented Dickey Fuller (ADF) test. The various tests for the order of integration in panel data series are all extensions of the ADF procedure. The ADF specification is:

$$\Delta y_{it} = \alpha_i y_{it-1} + \sum_{j=1}^{\rho_i} \beta_{ij} \Delta y_{it-1} + \delta d_{it} + \epsilon_{it} \qquad (2.3)$$

where d_{it} represents the deterministic component. When $\alpha_i = 0$, then the variable y_{it} has a unit root for the individual unit i. When $\alpha_i < 1$, then the variable y_{it} is stationary.

Broadly, there are two generations of panel unit root tests. The Levin, Lin, Chu (Levin et al. 2002) test (LLC), Fisher type tests, Im, Pesaran and Shin (Im et al. 2003) test, and Maddala and Wu (1999) belong to the first generation test, which assumes cross-sectional independence across the individual units. The second-generation test allowed for cross-sectional dependence or correlation among the various units. The Pesaran (2007) test for panel unit root is one of the frequently applied second-generation tests which make use of the common factor model framework. This paper applies the Pesaran (2007) test of unit root. A simple dynamic model with cross-sectional dependence is considered:

$$y_{i,t} = (1 - \partial_i)d_i + \partial_i y_{i,t-1} + u_{it} \qquad (2.4)$$

where d_i is the deterministic component, y_{i0} is the initial values, and the u_{it}, disturbance term, follows a one-factor structure given by

$$u_{it} = \delta_i f_t + \varepsilon_{it} \qquad (2.5)$$

In which ε_{it} is the individual specific error and f_t is the unobserved common factor. Eqs. (2.4) and (2.5) can be written as

$$\Delta y_{it} = \alpha_i + \beta_i y_{i,t-1} + \delta_i f_t + \varepsilon_{it} \qquad (2.6)$$

where $\alpha_i = (1 - \partial_i)d_i$, $\beta_i = -(1 - \partial_i)$, and $\Delta y_{it} = y_{it} - y_{i,t-1}$. Pesaran (2007) proposes the following unit root hypothesis:

$$H_O : \beta_i = 0 \text{ for all } i$$

$$H_1 : \beta_i < 0, \quad = 1, \dots, N_1, \beta_i = 0, i = N_1 + 1, N_1 + 2, \dots, N$$

assuming that N_1/N is the fraction of the individual cross-sectional units that are stationary.

The idiosyncratic shocks, ε_{it}, the unobserved common factor f_t, and the coefficient of the unobserved common factor δ_i are independently distributed for all i. In testing for unit root, Pesaran (2007) proposes t-ratio based on the ordinary least squares (OLS) estimate of $\beta_i(\widehat{\beta}_i)$ by augmenting the individual ADF regressions with the cross-sectional averages of lagged levels and differences of the individual series:

$$\Delta Y_{i,t} = \alpha_i + \beta_i Y_{i,t-1} + \gamma_i \bar{Y}_{t-1} + \delta_i \Delta \bar{Y}_t + \epsilon_{i,t} \tag{2.7}$$

where $\bar{Y}_t = \frac{1}{N} \sum_{i=1}^{N} Y_{i,t}$, $\Delta \bar{Y}_t = \frac{1}{N} \sum_{i=1}^{N} \Delta Y_{i,t}$, and $\epsilon_{i,\,t}$ is the error term.

2.3.3 Granger Causality Test

Following Holtz-Eakin et al. (1988), a bivariate panel VAR model is considered:

$$G(FDI)_{it} = \alpha_{11} + \sum_{i=1}^{T_{11}} \beta_{11i} G(FDI)_{i,t-1} + \sum_{j=1}^{T_{12}} \beta_{12j} G(BSD)_{i,t-j} + v_{12t} \tag{2.8}$$

$$G(BSD)_{it} = \alpha_{21} + \sum_{i=1}^{T_{21}} \beta_{21i} G(BSD)_{i,t-1} + \sum_{j=1}^{T_{22}} \beta_{22j} G(FDI)_{i,t-j} + v_{22t} \tag{2.9}$$

where G(FDI) and G(BSD) represent the growth of the ratio of FDI to GDP and banking sector development indicators [measured by three variables, growth of the ratio of liquid liabilities to GDP, G(LL/GDP); growth of the ratio of private sector credit to GDP, G(C/GDP); growth of the asset structure of the banking sector, G (CCA)], respectively. T is the lag order, α is the individual effect, and β's are the parameters of interest, v_t is the error term. Using Eqs. (2.8) and (2.9), Table 2.2 summarizes the various null and alternate hypotheses concerning the causal relationship between the growth of FDI and BSD.

Table 2.2 Hypotheses tested in this study

Causal flow of interest	Null hypothesis
G(CCA) => G(FDI/GDP)	G(CCA) does not Granger-cause G(FDI/GDP)
G(C/GDP) => G(FDI/GDP)	G(C/GDP) does not Granger-cause G(FDI/GDP)
G(LL/GDP) => G(FDI/GDP)	G(LL/GDP) does not Granger-cause G(FDI/GDP)
G(FDI/GDP) => G(CCA)	G(FDI/GDP) does not Granger-cause G(CCA)
G(FDI/GDP) => G(C/GDP)	G(FDI/GDP) does not Granger-cause G(C/GDP)
G(FDI/GDP) => G(LL/GDP)	G(FDI/GDP) does not Granger-cause G(LL/GDP)

G(FDI/GDP) measures the growth of the ratio of foreign direct investment (FDI) to gross domestic product (GDP). G(CCA) measures the growth of the ratio of total bank assets. G(LL/GDP) measures the growth of the ratio of liquid liabilities to GDP. G(C/GDP) measures the growth of the ratio of private sector credit to GDP

Table 2.3 Descriptive statistics

Variable	Obs	Mean	Std. dev.	Min	Max
English West Africa					
G(CCA)	104	0.07	0.15	−0.27	0.88
G(C/GDP)	104	0.05	0.14	−0.22	0.5
G(FDI/GDP)	104	0.88	7.48	−3.63	75.63
G(LL/GDP)	104	0.05	0.1	−0.25	0.45
French West Africa					
G(CCA)	208	0.01	0.08	−0.25	0.53
G(C/GDP)	208	0.02	0.13	−0.32	0.69
G(FDI/GDP)	208	−1.52	27.88	−371.44	62.93
G(LL/GDP)	208	0.03	0.09	−0.3	0.28

Note: GFDI/GDP measures the growth of the ratio of foreign direct investment (FDI) to gross domestic product (GDP). GCCA measures the growth of the ratio of total bank assets. GLL/GDP measures the growth of the ratio of liquid liabilities to GDP. GC/GDP measures the growth of the ratio of private sector credit to GDP

Table 2.4 Cross-sectional dependence test

| | English West Africa | | French West Africa | |
Variable	CD-test	*p*-Value	CD-test	*p*-Value
G(CCA)	3.43	0	10.76	0
G(C/GDP)	2.8	0.01	8.03	0
G(FDI/GDP)	1.57	0.12	0.54	0.59
G(LL/GDP)	2.96	0	4.76	0

Note: The null hypothesis assumes cross-section independence. *p*-values close to zero indicate the presence of cross-section dependence. G(FDI/GDP) measures the growth of the ratio of foreign direct investment (FDI) to gross domestic product (GDP). G(CCA) measures the growth of the ratio of total bank assets. G(LL/GDP) measures the growth of the ratio of liquid liabilities to GDP. G(C/GDP) measures the growth of the ratio of private sector credit to GDP Significant at 5%, Significant at 1%

2.4 Empirical Results

Table 2.3 shows the summary statistics of the variables chosen for this study. There is high variability in EWA compared to FWA except for the growth in FDI/GDP with 7.48 and 27.88 standard deviations, respectively. FWA experienced a considerable decline in growth of FDI/GDP of 371.44% compared to a relatively marginal decline of 3.63 in EWA for the period under study. The panel data in both regions are balanced (104 observations in EWA and 208 observations in FWA).

The mean values of the variables are higher in EWA than FWA. Especially, G(FDI/GDP) is 0.88 in EWA and −1.52 in FWA, which indicates that on an average, there seems to be disinvestment in FWA.

Table 2.5 Panel unit root test

Variable	English West Africa			French West Africa		
	Statistic	P-value	Decision	Statistic	P-value	Decision
G(CCA)	−3.59	0.00[***]	I(0)	−3.45	0.00[***]	I(0)
G(C/GDP)	−4.22	0.00[***]	I(0)	−3.64	0.00[***]	I(0)
G(FDI/GDP)	−6.94	0.00[***]	I(0)	−3.58	0.00[***]	I(0)
G(LL/GDP)	−3.30	0.00[***]	I(0)	−3.65	0.00[***]	I(0)

Note: Null hypothesis assumes that all series are non-stationary
The alternative hypothesis assumes that only some of the series are stationary. Variables with cross-section dependence are estimated using Pesaran (2007) CD unit root test, else the Im, Pesaran and Shin (Im et al. 2003) test is used. I(0) represents stationarity at level. The deterministic term: Constant. G(FDI/GDP) measures the growth of the ratio of foreign direct investment (FDI) to gross domestic product (GDP). G(CCA) measures the growth of the ratio of total bank assets. G(LL/GDP) measures the growth of the ratio of liquid liabilities to GDP. G(C/GDP) measures the growth of the ratio of private sector credit to GDP. [***]Significant at 1%

Table 2.6 Granger causality test

Causality between G(CCA), G(C/GDP), G(FDI/GDP), G(LL/GDP)					
	Variables	G(CCA)	G(C/GDP)	G(FDI/GDP)	G(LL/GDP)
English West Africa	G(CCA)	–	0.28	0.0001[***]	0.36
	G(C/GDP)	0.97	–	0.008[***]	0.99
	G(FDI/GDP)	0.64	0.024[**]	–	0.8
	G(LL/GDP)	0.006[***]	0.0016[***]	0[***]	–
French West Africa	G(CCA)	–	0[***]	0.0001[***]	0[***]
	G(C/GDP)	0.11	–	0.0^{2**}	0.0014[***]
	G(FDI/GDP)	0.29	0.35	–	0.045[**]
	G(LL/GDP)	0.03[**]	0.003[***]	0.095[*]	–

Note: Row and column variables indicate dependent and independent variables, respectively, in the Granger causality model. G(FDI/GDP) measures the growth of the ratio of foreign direct investment (FDI) to gross domestic product (GDP). G(CCA) measures the growth of the ratio of total bank assets. G(LL/GDP) measures the growth of the ratio of liquid liabilities to GDP. G(C/GDP) measures the growth of the ratio of private sector credit to GDP. [*]Significant at 10%, [**]Significant at 5%, [***]Significant at 1%

Table 2.4 shows the results of the cross-sectional dependence test. The *p*-values corresponding to G(CCA), G(C/GDP), and G(LL/GDP) indicate a rejection of the null hypothesis of cross-sectional independence in both EWA and FWA. The exception is G(FDI/GDP) with a p-value greater than 0.05; hence the null hypothesis cannot be rejected. The Pesaran Cross-sectional Augmented Dickey Fuller (CADF) test is to test for the presence of unit root in the variables except for G(FDI/GDP) where the Im, Pesaran and Shin Im et al. (2003) test is used.

The panel unit root results reported in Table 2.5 indicate that all the series are stationary at level for both EWA and FWA.

Given that the variables are stationary at level, the Granger causality tests are applied. The results are presented in Table 2.6. A bivariate vector autoregression (VAR) model consisting of Eqs. (2.8) and (2.9) is estimated using OLS and then the standard Wald test is applied to check the direction of causality. From Table 2.6, in the EWA region, Granger causality runs from G(CCA) to G(FDI/GDP), from G (C/GDP) to G(FDI/GDP), and from G(LL/GDP) to G(FDI/GDP) at the 1% significance level. Granger causality also runs from G(FDI/GDP) to G(C/GDP). The results indicate that bidirectional causality exists only between G(FDI/GDP) and G (C/GDP). Intuitively, the growth of credit extended to the private sector [G(C/GDP)] induces the growth of FDI flows (G(FDI/GDP)) into the EWA region.

Similarly, the growth of FDI flows (G(FDI/GDP)) into countries in EWA induces the growth of credit to the private sector. In the case of FWA, a unidirectional Granger causality runs only from all the banking sector development variables to growth in FDI inflows except the growth of liquid liabilities that has bidirectional causality with FDI flows.

Levin (2005) notes that among all the three measures of financial intermediation (liquid liabilities, total banking sector assets, and private credit), private credit is a direct and efficient measure of financial intermediation. For the reason that it solely measures credit to the private sector as opposed to other sectors such as public enterprises and government agencies, unlike total banking sector asset that includes central banks allocation of savings and liquid liabilities that include the interest-bearing liabilities of non-financial institutions. A significant difference between private credit and liquid liabilities is that the former measures actual financial intermediation, whereas the later measures capacity to intermediate. Hence the bidirectional causality between G(FDI/GDP) and G(C/GDP) in EWA indicates that the growth in FDI flows is induced by a stronger financial development relative to FWA, whereas the bidirectional causality between G(FDI/GDP) and G(LL/GDP) is induced from a weak financial development.

2.5 Conclusion

This paper examines the nature of the causal relationship between FDI and BSD in French West Africa (eight countries considered) and English West African countries (four countries considered). The findings suggest that BSD has an impact on FDI in both EWA and FWA. However, the impact of BSD seems to be stronger in EWA than in FWA since bidirectional causality exists between FDI/GDP and private credit in the former and between FDI/GDP and LL/GDP in the latter. This is in line with Chen et al. (2015) and Levin (2005), who found that financial development measured by private credit to GDP ratio positively and significantly influences the location of foreign affiliates to host countries. From the results, it follows that countries in West Africa, especially the French West African region should reform their financial regulations to deepen financial intermediation.

References

Abimbola, N. L., & Oludiran, A. S. (2018). Major determinants of foreign direct investment in the west African economic and monetary region. *Iranian Economic Review, 22*(1), 121–162.

Adam, A. M., & Tweneboah, G. (2009). Foreign direct investment and stock market development: Ghana's evidence. *International Research Journal of Finance and Economics, 26*, 178–185.

Alfaro, L., Chanda, A., Kalemli-Ozcan, S., & Sayek, S. (2004). FDI and economic growth: The role of local financial markets. *Journal of International Economics, 64*(1), 89–112.

Anyanwu, J. C. (2012), Why does foreign direct investment go where it goes? New evidence from African countries. *Annals of Economics and Finance, 13*(2), 433–470.

Anyanwu, J. C., & Yameogo, N. D. (2015). What drives foreign direct investments into West Africa? An empirical investigation. *African Development Review, 27*(3), 199–215.

Barro, R. J., & Sala-i-Martin, X. (2003). The diffusion of technology. In *Economic Growth* (pp. 349–380). The MIT Press.

Baltagi, B. H. (2008). Forecasting with panel data. *Journal of Forecasting, 27*, 153–173. https://doi.org/10.1002/for.1047

Bilir, K. L., Chor, D., & Manova, K. (2019). Host-country financial development and multinational activity. *European Economic Review, 115*, 192–220.

Chen, Y., Gao, Y., Ge, Y., & Li, J. (2015). Regional financial development and foreign direct investment. *Urban Studies, 52*(2), 358–373.

Desbordes, R., & Wei, S. J. (2017). The effects of financial development on foreign direct investment. *Journal of Development Economics, 127*, 153–168.

Feinberg, S., & Phillips, G. (2004). Growth, capital market development and competition for resources within MNCs. *NBER working paper.*

Gebrehiwot, A., Esfahani, N., & Sayim, M. (2016). The relationship between FDI and financial market development: The case of the sub-Saharan African region. *International Journal of Regional Development, 3*(1), 2373–9851.

Holtz-Eakin, D., Newey, W., & Rosen, H. S. (1988). Estimating vector autoregressions with panel data. *Econometrica, 56*, 1371–1395.

Huang, Y. (2011). *Determinants of financial development.* New York: Palgrave Macmillan.

Im, K. S., Pesaran, M. H., & Shin, Y. (2003). Testing for unit roots in heterogeneous panels. *Journal of Econometrics, 115*, 53–74.

IMF. (2016). *Financial development in sub-Saharan Africa, promoting inclusive and sustainable growth.* Washington, DC: IMF.

Levin, A., Lin, C. F., & Chu, C. S. (2002). Unit root tests in panel data: Asymptotic and finite-sample properties. *Journal of Econometrics, 108*, 1–24.

Levin, R. (2005). Finance and growth: Theory and evidence. In P. Aghion & S. Durlauf (Eds.), *Handbook of economic growth* (Vol. 1, pp. 865–934). Elsevier.

Maddala, G. S., & Wu, S. (1999). A comparative study of unit root tests with panel data and a new simple test. *Oxford Bulletin of Economics and Statistics, 61*, 631–652.

Musa, S. U., & Ibrahim, M. (2014). Stock market development, foreign direct investment, and macroeconomic stability: Evidence from Nigeria. *Research Journal of Finance and Accounting, 5*, 258–264.

OlugBenga, A. A., & Grace, O. O. (2015). Impact of foreign direct investment on Nigerian capital market development. *International Journal of Academic Research in Accounting, Finance and Management Sciences, 5*, 103–108.

Otchere, I., Soumaré, I., & Yourougou, P. (2016). FDI and financial market development in Africa. *The World Economy, 39*, 651–678.

Pesaran, H. M. (2007). A simple panel unit root test in the presence of cross-section dependence. *Journal of Applied Econometrics, 22*, 265–312.

Pesaran, H. M., & Tosetti, E. (2011). Large panels with common factors and spatial correlation. *Journal of Econometrics, 161*, 182–202.

Soumaré, I., & Tchana Tchana, F. (2015). Causality between FDI and financial market development: Evidence from emerging markets. *The World Bank Economic Review, 29*, S205–S216.

UNCTAD. (2018). *World investment report*. Geneva: United Nations Publication.

Chapter 3
Impact of FDI and TRIPS on the Absorptive Capacity of Manufacturing Firms in India

Sunil Kumar Ambrammal and P. Baiju

3.1 Introduction

The general theory of Foreign Direct Investment (FDI) that discusses its impact on the host country may not be applicable to developing countries, as in the same way as it is applicable to the developed nations, due to the substantiate differences in the innovative nature of these two sets of countries (World Bank 1997). In developing countries, domestic enterprises are relatively small and technologically backward. These countries are also different from the developed ones in such aspects like the degree of protection, market size, and policy incentives. The entry of FDI into developing countries and its effect (both positive and negative), therefore, seems to be different from what is befalling in developed countries. Studying the impact of FDI on the host country has been started early in the 1960s and that particular industrial organization theory explored the marginal impact of FDI on the factors of production (MacDougall 1960). Since then, numerous studies have been conducted on the various issues of FDI in host countries and many of them are searching the reason for their investment in other countries (Caves 1971; Dunning 1973; Kindleberger 1969). Most of the results argue that firms entering into a host country with superior technology in production, process, management or marketing skills that distinguish them with local (domestic) firms. These superior skills help them to procure benefits from the host country by creating an artificial monopoly. It is interesting to see that a lot of empirical studies have come up with the effect of FDI on host countries. Traditional trade theories argue that FDI can bring direct benefits like factor reward, employment, and capital flows to the host countries

S. K. Ambrammal (✉) · P. Baiju
Department of Humanities and Sciences, National Institute of Technology Goa, Ponda, Goa, India
e-mail: sunilkumar@nitgoa.ac.in

A. K. Mishra et al. (eds.), *Advances in Innovation, Trade and Business*,
Contributions to Management Science,
https://doi.org/10.1007/978-3-030-60354-0_3

(MacDougall 1960; Lipsey et al. 1995). On the other hand, industrial organization theorists mainly concentrate on the indirect benefits or the externalities created by multinational corporations (MNCs) on the host countries. These existing studies, however, did not consider the effect of Intellectual property rights (IPR) protection on the inflow of FDI and its contribution to the host country. The present study would like to consider both the arguments (traditional and industrial organization) by incorporating the direct and indirect effects of FDI on the host country in the wake of enhanced IPR protection in India.

3.2   Theoretical Background on the Interconnection Between FDI, IPR, and Technological

Firms in the twenty-first century are facing rigorous competition from their rivals with strategic discontinuities and unpredictable environmental changes (Hitt 1998). To survive, firms must learn how to minimize the negative effects of discontinuities and uncertainty while simultaneously achieving essential capabilities to explore environmental opportunities (Lei et al. 1996). Scholars believed that intellectual capabilities, rather than physical assets, are the major source for competitive advantage as contemporary competition is becoming more knowledge-based (Subramaniam and Venkatraman 1999). To maintain the competitive advantage and generate value, firms' need to invest in the knowledge-based resources in a way that they must be in a position to generate, diffuse, and apply the generated knowledge for their existence (Hoopes and Postrel 1999; Kogut and Zander 1996). Strengthening of IPR through TRIPs regulation is mainly aiming to safeguard these intellectual creations, and which is globally benefitting to developed nations due to their dominance in the control of intellectual property (Lippoldt 2006). Developing countries, on the other hand, are expected to benefit through FDI and technology transfer as the higher IPR provides a conducive environment for doing R&D and business in such nations (Asid et al. 2004). The "product cycle" model in international economics explained how North-South FDI has stimulated under the strengthened IPR reforms. Later, Helpman (1992) extended the model by introducing several variants of North-South trade and FDI by arguing that the FDI inflows result for the North-South Wage conversion. In reality, however, these wage conversion doesn't happen and at the same time, the lowest wages in the South become the key determinant for the FDI. A stronger IPR protection in the South, on the other hand, raises the imitation cost of Southern firms and thereby reduces the threat of imitation. This allows MNEs to shift their production centers into South and relocated Northern resources towards South for the innovative activities (Lai 1998).

Growth of a nation is accompanied by technological change and the new entrepreneurial firms are considered as the channels for this technological change (Aghion and Howitt 1992; Klette and Kortum 2004). By technological change, this study refers to the microaspect of the technical progress which seek to explain the process of technical change that consists of all knowledge creating activities of research, invention, and development, together with the process of application of new knowledge into the system in firms and industries (Kennedy and Thirlwall 1972). A firm can gain access to technological knowledge through two sources: primary/internal and acquisitive/external (Hitt et al. 2000). Besides their capability to develop knowledge, firms can acquire it from outside the organization's boundaries and then diffuse it. Mere receiving of new ideas and techniques, however, does not ensure any technical gain, which further depends on the absorptive capacity. Absorptive capacity refers to the firm's ability to recognize the value of external information, assimilate and apply it to the commercial end (Cohen and Levinthal 1990). In a developing country context, we can argue that the gaining of technical progress is a process whereby an economy is exposed to higher technology business, product, and services through foreign trade, Foreign Direct Investment (FDI), and other channels like licensing. Besides these forms, a typical channel of technology transfer is the imitation.

Irrespective of the channel, the most required condition for acquiring foreign knowledge is their absorptive capacity which is further influenced by the strength of Intellectual Property Protection in the country. As a founder member of both WTO and GATT, India was bound to establish an Intellectual Property (IP) law that is in line with the TRIPs mandate and consequently the IP regime of the country has been revised several times since 1995. As a result of series of changes made in their IP laws, the country is now compatible with international IP laws by making solid steps in stiffening the IP rights, especially a patent system, in the country. The present IP regime is likely to bring technological advances in line with its global commitments. The decision to implement the same level of IPR irrespective of a country's level of development, however, has been questioned by several researchers and policymakers (Branstetter et al. 2007). The reason is that the same level of IP may not work in the same direction both for developed and developing nations. The nature and pace of innovation are different in both these two sets of countries and hence, it can be argued that developing countries need imitative rather than innovative entrepreneurs. The argument in favor of higher IPR in developing countries mainly concentrates on the technological advancement which is expected to arrive through FDI, trade, and licensing. Among them, FDI is considered as the most typical channel for the technology upgradation in the host country. This inflow of technology is likely to reduce the technological gap between the two sets of countries. Owing to the positive and negative impacts of tighter IPR in the low-income countries, the net effect is still unclear. The present study, therefore, would like to see the impact of FDI and higher IPR on the technical advancement of India, which is measured through the absorptive capacity of firms. Since there are numerous versions and definitions for technical progress (TP), the study would like to disintegrate the TP into two, i.e. technology absorption (ACAP) and technology creation (CREAT).[1] The research question here is how far the implementation of the

---

[1]The present study is, however, considering only the first component, ACAP for the estimation.

TRIPs mandate in developing countries helps them to improve their technological base of India through FDI. Generally, acquiring absorptive capacity is a pre-requisite for receiving technology and build further on it. However, none of the theory says that the so-called ACAP is constant, rather it is variable. Therefore, we can argue that firms' may enhance their ACAP according to their needs. As and when more and more foreign investment inflow began, firms may respond by enhancing their ACAP. Therefore, we have all the reasons to believe that ACAP changes according to the years and amount of foreign technology that they receive. In this regard, we have formulated the following research objectives.

3.3 Objectives

The broader objective of the study is to evaluate the impact of FDI and a higher level of IPR on the absorptive capacity (ACAP) of firms (sector) in developing countries with special reference to India. The study initially tests the individual impact of FDI and IPR on the ACAP and later we investigate the join impact of these factors on the ACAP. The specific objectives are detailed below:

- To estimate the impact of IPR on the absorptive capacity of firms in India.
- To estimate the impact of FDI on the absorptive capacity of firms in India.
- To analyze the joint impact of FDI and IPR on the absorptive capacity of firms in India.

3.4 Methodology and Data

The study would like to estimate the impact of FDI and IPR on the technological activities, especially on the absorptive capacity of firms in India. Technological activities comprised of both technology absorption and technology creation where absorptive capacity is regarded as an essential pre-requisite for creative utilization of technology received from the firms from abroad, while technology creation is an outcome of the application of received technology in a proper manner. In this paper, we are considering only the absorptive capacity aspect of foreign fund. FDI, since it is not available at the firm level, is collected at the industry level. The data is collected from the Department of Industrial Policy and Promotion (DIPP) archives. FDI data, therefore, summarized for each industry according to the concordance between DIPP 92-4 digit sectors and NIC 2008 classification. We have constructed the variable ACAP according to Kostopoulos et al. (2011). They formulated a principle component based on R&D, employees with bachelor degree, dummy variable for doing consistent R&D, and a dummy variable for training activities carried out by the firms. We have not constructed a principle component as most of our variables R&D intensity, fee for technical knowhow (TKH), and expenses incurred for training the personnel's (TEX) are in the same line. Instead of principle component, we have formulated a weighted average of the ACAP with 0.5, 0.3, and 0.2 weightage for the R&D, TKH, and TEX, respectively.

Since the aim of the study is to identify the relationship between FDI and ACAP, we have considered all the sectors where FDI data is available. After the cleaning process, we have data for 44 sectors ranging from 2007 to 2017.[2] Data on the firm level is collected from the Center for Monitoring Indian Economy (CMIE) database and later they have converted to Industry level as discussed above. Another variable, which would have an impact on the ACAP, is the intellectual property protection in the host country. Hence, we considered IPR score prepared by International Property Alliance as another determining factor for the ACAP (IPRI). We have considered advertising expenditure (ADEX) as a proxy for the prevailing competition in the sector. We assume as competition increases, firms may improve their technical base by creating absorptive capacity. To measure the size of the industry, we consider deflated salaries and wages (SIZE). As plant size and production increases, it is believed that, they may have to recruit more personal and the same can be capture through the payment made to the respective employees. Another factor that contributes to the technological improvement is the capital available with the firms. Therefore, we have considered total capital imported (CAPIMP) as a controlling variable in the model. It is argued that firms' with foreign activity will have more tendency to upgrade their technical capacity as they have to face stiff competition in the international market than the firms with only domestic activities.

3.4.1 Econometric Model

ACAP is not generated in 1 day or in 1 year, rather it is continuous process. Successive technological efforts are needed to build upon their capacity. Hence, there are all reasons to believe that the previous year's ACAP is also influencing the current year's capacity. The present model therefore considered previous years ACAP also as an explanatory variable in the model. The link between FDI, IPR, and technology creation can be estimated as follows:

$$ACAP = f(\ ACAP_{i-1}, FDI, IPR, X_{it}, U_{it}) \tag{3.1}$$

$$ACAP = f(ACAP_{i-1},\ FDI, X_{it}, U_{it}) \tag{3.2}$$

$$ACAP = f(ACAP_{i-1},\ IPR, X_{it}, U_{it}) \tag{3.3}$$

---

[2]FDI data is available for 44 sectors for some years and 63 sectors for the remaining years. For the continuity, we have focused on 44 sectors which is further based on the concordance available with the DIPP.

Table 3.1 Summary statistics of the variables

Variable	Obs	Mean	Std. dev.	Min	Max
ACAP	435	501.4434	1329.391	0	9807.006
IPRI	435	5.432598	0.201372	5.15	5.83
SIZE	435	113918.7	238836.7	0	2,110,012
SALES	435	1,579,585	3,127,126	0	2.38E+07
ADEXP	435	10812.68	19685.86	0	172645.4
FDI	435	725.2617	1303.784	0.1	8684.07
IMCAPG	435	22288.62	48128.82	0	336530.1

Table 3.2 Correlation matrix

	ACAP	FDI	IPRI	Size	Sales	ADEXP	IMCAPG
ACAP	1						
FDI	0.5466	1					
IPRI	−0.044	−0.0322	1				
SIZE	0.7319	0.6466	−0.0394	1			
SALES	0.1295	0.3385	−0.0304	0.3608	1		
ADEXP	0.4729	0.5085	−0.0755	0.4028	0.1217	1	
IMCAPG	0.1138	0.3542	0.0149	0.3085	0.7326	0.1093	1

where ACAP is the technology absorption, X_{it} is the summated firm specific variable for the industry "i" for the "t" period, U_{it} is the un observed firm specific as well as industry specific characteristics. We have three separate equations; the first one measures the joint effect FDI and IPR in the creation of ACAP, whereas the second and third measure the impact of individual effects of FDI and IPR.

Since we have included lagged values of dependent variable in the estimation process, our model represents a dynamic panel data model. We have therefore, considered Arellano and Bond (1991) GMM estimator to evaluate the dependence of explanatory variables on the ACAP. GMM estimator is considered as one of the efficient estimators in the presence of endogeneity (Baum et al. 2002). As suggested by Hansen (1982), when a model is facing heteroscedasticity, researchers can apply the GMM.

3.5 Result and Discussion

Begin with; we present the summary statistics and correlation matrix among the variable through Tables 3.1 and 3.2, respectively. Table 3.1 shows that we have 435 observations across the variables, with minimum zero (0) value for most of the variables. The percentage of zero is, however, very less and can be negligible. For example, we got a zero value for sales only for 2 years. Similar case is applicable to

Table 3.3 Joint effect of IPR and FDI on the ACAP

ACAP	1	2
L1.ACAP	0.425 (4.64)***	0.354 (7.57)***
FDI		0.0057 (0.19)
L1.FDI	0.0069 (0.2)	
IPRI	−35.434 (0.31)	−130.35(−0.89)
ADEXP	−0.021 (−2.22)**	−0.016 (−2.87)**
SIZE	0.0072 (7.58)***	0.0069 (10.33)***
CAPIMP	−0.0034(−0.86)	−0.0016(−1.03)
Constant	65.869(0.09)	542.163(0.66)
# Observations	336	378
Number of groups	42	42
Wald Chi2	chi2(35) 234.27(0.000)	chi2(44) 292.34(0.000)

Note: *** & **, respectively, for 1 and 5 percentage significantly

all the variables presented here. Since most of the variables have been considered in its original form for the summary, is has shown huge standard deviation for most of the variables.

Table 3.2 represents the correlation matrix among the variables, where none of the variables are highly correlated (the highest reported correlation is 0.73). The problem of multicollinearity generally exists if any pair-wise correlation between two explanatory variable exceeds 0.80 (Gujarati 2009). We consider this rule of thumb and assume that there is not any issue of multicollinearity in the present dataset.

Initially we have estimated the joint effect of IPR and FDI on the absorptive capacity of firms in India. The results are produced in Table 3.3. Column (1) uses the lagged FDI, whereas the column (2) employs current value of FDI for the estimation. We have applied the panel dynamic model for including the effect of previous years ACAP on the present. It is seen that there is an indication of positive influence, even though the coefficient is not significant, of FDI on the ACAP. While including the lagged value of FDI, we have seen that the coefficient is improved by 0.001 units. It is observed that, another variable of interest IPR produces a negative impact on the capacity, though the coefficient does not produce significant results. What is more important is the positive association between industry size and ACAP. Industries with bigger size firms invest to improve their ACAP under the tight IPR and higher FDI inflow. Industry competition, measured through advertising expenditure, shows a negative impact on the ACAP. This supports the Schumpeterian arguments that an increase in competition decreases the innovative effects of laggard firms (Aghion et al. 2005). This is probably because of the reduction in postinnovation profits/rent of laggard firms due to the highest level of competition and thereby reduces the incentive to innovate.

In the next step, in Table 3.4, we have estimated the individual effects of FDI (through columns 3 & 4) and IPR (through columns 5 & 6) on the ACAP of Indian manufacturing firms in India. The results show that irrespective of the models and

Table 3.4 Impact of FDI & IPR independently on ACAP

ACAP	3	4	5	6
L1.ACAP	0.351 (7.53)***	0.425 (8.42)***	0.353 (7.56)***	0.349 (7.43)***
FDI	0.0056 (0.19)	-NA-	-NA-	-NA-
L1.FDI	-NA-	0.0071 (0.24)	-NA-	-NA-
IPRI	-NA-	-NA-	−132.59 (−0.9)	−9592.36 (−1.31)
IPRI^2	-NA-	-NA-	-NA-	868.26 (−2.96)
ADEXP	−0.0157 (−2.79)**	−0.021 (−3.52)***	−0.016 (−2.89)**	−0.017 (10.58)***
SIZE	0.007 (10.54)***	0.007 (10.24)***	0.007 (10.5)***	0.007 (−1.13)
CAPIMP	−0.0016 (−1.02)	−0.0034 (−1.76)	−0.002 (−1.03)	−0.002 (1.29)
Constant	−180.35 (−2.33)**	−130.28 (−1.53)	556.28 (0.68)	26290.24 (1.31)
Observations	378	336	378	378
Groups	42	42	42	42
# instruments	50	41	50	51
Wald chi2(5)	427.67 (0.00)	397.71 (0.00)	428.62 (0.00)	427.37 (0.00)

Note: *** & ** respectively for 1percentage and 5 percentage significantly

restriction, lagged ACAP and size of the industry, which measured through salaries and wages, shows positive and significant impact on the ACAP of the sectors. However, when we introduce the squared value of IPR, size of the industry shows insignificant results. Industry competition, measured through the advertising expenditure, shows a negative impact on the ACAP. This supports the Schumpeterian arguments that an increase in competition decreases the innovative effects of laggard firms (Aghion et al. 2005). This is probably because of the reduction in postinnovation profits/rent of laggard firms due to the highest level of competition and thereby reduces the incentive to innovate.

The key variable FDI and its lagged form show a positive indication towards the enhancement of ACAP due to the improved FDI Inflow. This indicates that, formation of ACAP is a continuous process and it endures even after receiving the FDI from abroad. IPR, on the other hand, shows a negative impact on the ACAP as the coefficients are insignificantly negative. The better argument for negative association between IPR and ACAP is that, in India, firms are promoting imitative innovation rather than creative innovation. These imitative innovation can grow much faster rate under a weak IPR regime. Hence, a strong IP regime induces an insignificant and negative relationship with ACAP.

3.6   Findings and Conclusion

The present study is testing the hypothesis that FDI necessitates the absorptive capacity of firms' in India on the assumption that ACAP is not only a pre-request, but also an outcome of the technology inflow. We find that the previous year ACAP is significantly contributes to the current year's capacity, but not the FDI. This supports our argument that ACAP is not constant over the years but gradually building over the previous year's capacity. Surprisingly we could not find the support of the FDI link to the ACAP. Probably FDI alone will not build the ACAP, rather we have to focus on the other modes of technology transfer including trade and licensing.

We find that the size of the firm is significantly contributing to the ACAP as it says that an increase in size of the firm produces a significant impact on the ACAP of firms. We shall argue that economies of scale help them to build the ACAP as it enables them to increase the cost-effectiveness among the firms. We also find that advertising really does not help for capacity formation, rather it may work only for the making of profit. It implies that in the long run advertising does not help firms' survival if they are not really focusing on the capacity building R&D oriented activities.

References

Aghion, P., Bloom, N., Blundell, R. W., Griffith, R., & Howitt, P. (2005). Competition and innovation: An inverted U relationship. *Quarterly Journal of Economics, 120*(2), 701–728.

Aghion, P., & Howitt, P. (1992). A model of growth through creative distruction. *Econometrica, 60* (2), 323–351. Retrieved from https://EconPapers.repec.org/RePEc:ecm:emetrp:v:60:y:1992:i:2: p:323-51.

Arellano, M., & Bond, S. (1991). Some tests of specification for panel data: Monte Carlo evidence and an application to employment equations. *The Review of Economic Studies, 58*(2), 277. https://doi.org/10.2307/2297968.

Asid, R., Yusof, Y. S., & Saiman, S. (2004). Impact of intellectual property protection, domestic market condition and R & D expenditure on foreign direct investment Inflow. Preliminary evidence in elected cross-countries data. *Munich Personal RePEc Archive Paper No. 1008.*

Baum, C. F., Mark, E. F., & Stillman, S. (2002). Instrumental variables and GMM: Estimation and testing, *Boston College Economics Working Papers 545*. Retrieved January 1, 2020, from http:// faculty.washington.edu/ezivot/econ583/ivreg2_bcwp545.pdf.

Branstetter, L., Fisman, R., Foley, C. F., & Saggi, K. (2007). *Intellectual property rights, imitation, and foreign direct investment: Theory and evidence (no. w13033)*. National Bureau of Economic Research. doi: https://doi.org/10.3386/w13033.

Caves, R. E. (1971). International corporations: The industrial economics of foreign investment. *Economica, 38*(149), 1–27. https://doi.org/10.2307/2551748.

Cohen, W. M., & Levinthal, D. A. (1990). Absorptive capacity: A new perspective on learning and innovation. *Administrative Science Quarterly, 35*(1), 128–152. https://doi.org/10.2307/ 2393553.

Dunning, J. H. (1973). The determinants of international production. *Oxford Economic Papers, 25* (3), 289–336.

Gujarati, D. N. (2009). Basic econometrics. Tata McGraw-Hill Education.

Hansen, L. (1982). Large sample properties of generalized method of moments estimators. *Econometrica, 50*(3), 1029–1054.

Helpman, E. (1992). Innovation, imitation, and intellectual property rights, *National Bureau of Economic Research, Working Paper 4081.* doi:https://doi.org/10.3386/w4081.

Hitt, M. A. (1998). Twenty-first-century organizations: Business firms, business schools, and the academy. *The Academy of Management Review, 23*(2), 218. https://doi.org/10.2307/259371.

Hitt, M. A., Ireland, R. D., & Lee, H. U. (2000). Technological learning, knowledge management, firm growth and performance: An introductory essay. *Journal of Engineering and Technology Management, 17*(3–4), 231–246. https://doi.org/10.1016/S0923-4748(00)00024-2.

Hoopes, D. G., & Postrel, S. (1999). Shared knowledge, 'glitches,' and product development performance. *Strategic Management Journal, 20*(9), 837–865. https://doi.org/10.1002/(SICI)1097-0266(199909)20:9<837::AID-SMJ54>3.0.CO;2-I.

Kennedy, C., & Thirlwall, A. P. (1972). Surveys in applied economics: technical progress. *The Economic Journal, 82*(325), 11–72. https://doi.org/10.2307/2230206.

Kindleberger, C. P. (1969). American business abroad. *The International Executive, 11*(2), 11–12.

Klette, T. J., & Kortum, S. (2004). Innovating firms and aggregate innovation. *Journal of Political Economy, 112*(5), 986–1018. https://doi.org/10.1086/422563.

Kogut, B., & Zander, U. (1996). What firms do? Coordination, identity, and learning. *Organization Science, 7*(5), 502–518. https://doi.org/10.1287/orsc.7.5.502.

Kostopoulos, K., Papalexandris, A., Papachroni, M., & Ioannou, G. (2011). Absorptive capacity, innovation, and financial performance. *Journal of Business Research, 64*(12), 1335–1343. https://doi.org/10.1016/j.jbusres.2010.12.005.

Lai, E. L. (1998). International intellectual property rights protection and the rate of product innovation. *Journal of Development Economics, 55*(1), 133–153. https://doi.org/10.1016/s0304-3878(97)00059-x.

Lei, D., Hitt, M., & Bettis, R. (1996). Dynamic core competences through meta-learning and strategic context. *Journal of Management, 22*, 549–570. https://doi.org/10.1016/s0149-2063(96)90024-0.

Lippoldt, D. (2006). Can stronger intellectual property rights boost trade, foreign direct investment and licensing in developing countries? Chapter 3. In M. P. Pugatch (Ed.), *The intellectual property debate*. Northampton, MA: Edward Elgar Publishing.

Lipsey, R. E., Blomstrom, M, & Ramstetter, E. (1995). Internationalized production in world output, *NBER Working Paper 5385.* doi: https://doi.org/10.3386/w5385.

MacDougall, G. D. A. (1960). The benefits and costs of private investment from abroad: A theoretical approach. *Economic Record, 36*, 13–35. https://doi.org/10.1111/j.1475-4932.1960.tb00491.x.

Subramaniam, M., & Venkatraman, N. (1999). *The influence of leveraging tacit overseas knowledge for global new product development capability. Dynamic strategy resources* (pp. 373–401). Oxford: Blackwell.

World Bank. (1997). *World development report 1997: The state in a changing world*. New York: Oxford University Press.

Chapter 4
The Trade Impact of Indian Anti-Dumping Measures on ASEAN-6 Countries

Pooja Verma

4.1 Introduction

Trade-war is the application of trade remedy measures (Anti-dumping, Countervailing, and Safeguard) to target the unfair imports growth of trading partners. Though gained momentum in recent years, it is not a novel phenomenon in international trade. Unarguably, Anti-dumping measures have remained the most popular trade remedies after the formalisation of the General Agreement on Tariffs and Trade in 1947. The promulgation of Anti-dumping as a legislation began with Canada in 1904. Later, New Zealand joined in 1905, Australia in 1906, the USA in 1916, and UK in 1921 Viner (1923). Due to the introduction of amendments to AD law in 1974 the USA, European Union, Australia, and Canada were the primary users of anti-dumping in the 1980–1990s with the USA only accounting for 28% of these cases Aggarwal (2003). The developing countries initiated only 11 cases of anti-dumping throughout the 1980s. The reason was that they maintained high levels of tariffs, quotas, and restrictive import licenses that made anti-dumping instrument superfluous. With the creation of the World Trade Organization in 1995 and subsequent trade liberalisation, the anti-dumping tool usage gained prominence amongst developing member countries to protect their domestic industries in the face of severe competition due to increased market access Moore & Zanardi (2009). The WTO provision on anti-dumping allows the member countries to protect their domestic industries from the injuries caused by foreign competitors by the virtue of the Article VI Bown (2008).As a result, the developing countries such as Brazil, China, and India have increasingly started to use these measures. India is the founding member of the General Agreement on Tariffs and Trade and the World Trade Organisation. It was neither a user of the anti-dumping mechanism nor

P. Verma (✉)
Department of Economics, Jamia Millia Islamia, New Delhi, India

© The Author(s), under exclusive license to Springer Nature Switzerland AG 2021
A. K. Mishra et al. (eds.), *Advances in Innovation, Trade and Business*,
Contributions to Management Science,
https://doi.org/10.1007/978-3-030-60354-0_4

Table 4.1 India's top 10 AD targets (1995–2015), World Trade Organisation (2016) AntiDumping Initiations and Measures by Member Countries

Target country	Anti-dumping initiations	Anti-dumping measures
China	174	162
European Union	56	53
Korea	56	52
Taiwan	55	53
United States	40	37
Thailand	39	35
Japan	33	30
Malaysia	27	18
Indonesia	26	24
Singapore	26	24
Other countries	220	69
Total	752	557

affected by anti-dumping actions until the 1990s. However, after the liberalisation of the economy in 1991, India has become a significant user of the anti-dumping Raju (2008).

According to WTO reports (2015), India emerged as the most massive user of the anti-dumping tool against all its trading partners from the period of 1995–2015. From the inception of the WTO until 2016, India accounted for 839 of the anti-dumping initiations out of 5286, i.e., 16% of the total, and it leads the tally of the traditional users such as the USA (606) and European Union (493) as well as new users Argentina (403) and Brazil (383) in filling anti-dumping petitions Blonigen & Prusa (2016). Regarding the final measures, it also leads with the highest success rate, i.e., in 74% of anti-dumping cases, resulted in final duties.

Table 4.1 lists top 10 countries that were targets of the Indian anti-dumping cases in the period 1995–2015. Besides traditional users, India's anti-dumping cases frequently targeted Asian region countries such as China, Republic of Korea, Taiwan, and ASEAN countries. Notably, India has imposed the highest no. of cases against China which is (23%) of the total Wu (2012). Other targets have been European Union (7.4%), Korea (7.4%), Taiwan (7.3%), USA (5.3%), Thailand (5.1%), and Japan (4.3%).

This article consists of six sections. Introduction is followed by literature review in Sect. 4.2. Section 4.3 presents objectives. Section 4.4 provides a historical overview of India ASEAN-6 trade. Section 4.5 examines the Indian AD case profile against ASEAN-6 industries. Data sources and methodology are discussed in Sect. 4.6. Section 4.7 discusses the empirical results. While, Sect. 4.8 presents conclusion.

4.2 Literature Review

Dumping of the goods denotes a situation when the product is sold in the exporting country at a price lower than its actual selling price in the home market of the exporter Viner (1923). Anti-dumping literature has been contributed by significant number of theoretical and empirical researches. The efficacy of anti-dumping on imports has been tested by analysing imports patterns over time on aggregated and disaggregated form of imports by dumping countries imports. Prusa (1996) examination of U.S. anti-dumping cases between 1980 and 1988 finds that trade destruction effect on named and non-named countries is equally significant for the withdrawn and terminated cases than cases which results in actual duty. Import diversion is substantial from the non-named countries only in cases with higher duties. On the other hand, Prusa (2001) re-examination of the trade effects of U.S. anti-dumping duties on value and quantities of imports for the period (1987–1997) finds that anti-dumping actions reduce the trade from named countries with little trade diversion.

Brenton's (2001) examination of EU anti-dumping cases finds the weak trade diversion. In contrast, Konings et al. (2001) study for EU anti-dumping cases for 1985–1990 finds significant import diversion from domestic EU market. In contrast to previous studies, his results underestimate the impact of EU anti-dumping. Many studies examine the use of developing countries anti-dumping policy. Some of these studies are noteworthy.

An important study by Kim and Kang (2017) empirically estimates the effect of anti-dumping duties levied by ASEAN countries for the period 2000–2010 using the ordinary least square regression. The regression estimates indicates that duties depress the trade from named and non-named countries but remain ambiguous about trade diversion from non-named countries. Although India has been the highest user of anti-dumping duties, there are very few empirical studies on India's anti-dumping policy.

Ganguli (2008) estimates the effects of Indian anti-dumping duties on all its trading partners for the entire period of (1992–2002). The study finds that AD duties distort the trade equivalently from the named as well as non-named countries. Concerning the impact of duties on non-named countries the study results claims insignificant trade diversion. Overall, his study finds the smaller trade effects due to the biased estimation procedure.

Aggarwal (2010) analysis of Indian anti-dumping cases for the period (1994–2001) finds that anti-dumping duties reduce the imports (value and volume) from named as well as non-named countries followed by an increase in the domestic prices. The study also finds weak evidence for trade diversion from non-named countries. The study further analysed the differential trade effects of anti-dumping duty on developed and developing countries and for market vs. non-market economies. The specification results point out that trade destruction is more severe for developing countries imports than developed countries. The result follows due to the insignificant decline in imports value and volume from both named and non-named developed countries in comparison to the developing countries.

Vandenbussche and Viegelahn (2013) examines the impact of Indian anti-dumping measures against Chinese imports during the great recession 2009–2010 by examining 13 anti-dumping cases. The study finds significant trade depressing effect of duties on imports from China. All of the studies find significant trade diversion due to the anti-dumping policy which makes anti-dumping policy highly successful in protecting domestic industries.

While enormous academic literature is existent that examine the trade effects of the anti-dumping on imports from all the countries, relatively few studies estimated the trade effects of anti-dumping actions against ASEAN Countries. Mah (1999) analysis of the U.S. anti-dumping cases against imports from six ASEAN countries briefly examines the trade pattern from the selected ASEAN countries and highlights the significance of trade balance and prominent industry role in initiating the anti-dumping cases. The study finds that U.S. ITC dumping margin criteria leads to the imposition of the highest number of duties against these countries. Cuyvers and Dumont (2005) empirical estimation for the impact of 12 EU anti-dumping cases on ASEAN countries imports value and volume for 1991–2001. The regression estimates point the significant effect of duties in reducing the trade and significant trade diversion from EU imports than non-EU imports. Despite the existence of vast literature on the trade effect of anti-dumping duties, the impact of developing countries anti-dumping measures on imports from ASEAN countries is less studied. The present study attempts to counter this limitation by examining the effect of anti-dumping measures on the fourth largest trade partner of India, i.e., ASEAN countries.

The lack of current academic literature concerning the broad effect of these anti-dumping measures on India's trade potential with this region has driven present empirical analysis. Notably, India has initiated 133 cases against these six countries which are 18% of the total cases. Further, this study also aims to examine the trade diversion from the countries not named.

4.3 Objective

The present study aims for empirical examination of India's Anti-dumping cases on ASEAN-6 imports for the period 1995–2015.

4.4 India-ASEAN trade

The Association of South East Asian Nation (ASEAN) is a regional inter-governmental organization, created on eighth August 1967 by the five countries Indonesia, Malaysia, Philippines, Singapore, and Thailand who signed the ASEAN declaration. Three Members such as Brunei (1985), Vietnam (1995), and Laos and Myanmar (1997) joined lately. ASEAN region has been an important trading partner after the adoption of the "Look East Policy" by India in 1991 Ahmed (2010). Formerly, India and ASEAN signed a framework Agreement—the Comprehensive Economic Cooperation Agreement (CECA)—on 8 October 2003. Finally, India and ASEAN signed the regional trade agreement in goods called the ASEAN–India Free Trade Area (AIFTA) on January 2010 to facilitate the free trade in goods Ministry of Commerce and Industry of India (2018(c)). India's partnership with ASEAN-4, i.e., Indonesia, Malaysia, Singapore, and Thailand are more significant than other countries from the ASEAN region. With the implementation of the Free trade area, these countries benefitted from the tariff concessions in large import categories.

Although, ASEAN is an important trading partner for India. The six-member countries (Indonesia, Malaysia, Thailand, Singapore, Philippines, and Vietnam) from this region have experienced rapid economic growth and development. In the year 2015, ASEAN's export to India remains 39100.8 million U.S. dollars and Imports at 19452.8 million U.S. dollars and total trade at 58553.5 million U.S. dollars. In terms of (percent share of total) exports from ASEAN stands at 3.3% and imports by ASEAN stands at 1.8% with positive trade balance of 2.8%. ASEAN India trade have grown steadily except east Asian crisis period. Surprisingly, ASEAN-6 accounts more than 90% of India's trade with ASEAN countries.

Figure 4.1 presents India's trade with ASEAN-6 countries. Thus, in the year 2015 these countries export share grown at 9.9% while import shares have grown at 8.9%. This pattern of increase in ASEAN-6 exports shares more than imports shares points the negative trade balance with these countries.

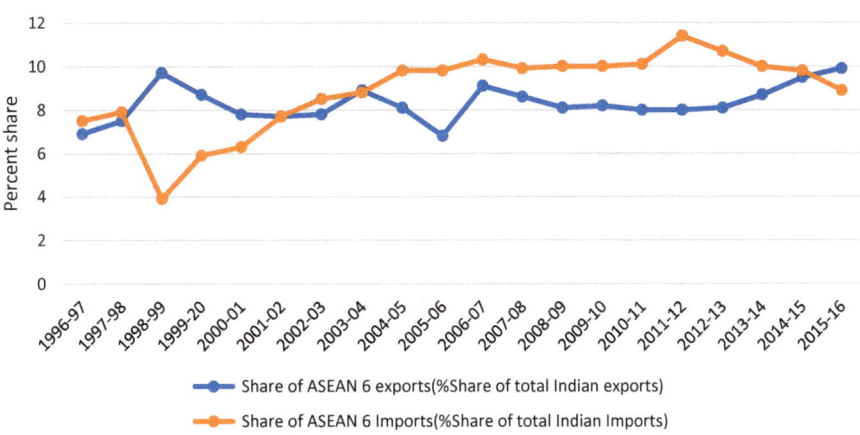

Fig. 4.1 India's export and import share with ASEAN-6 Ministry of Commerce & Industry of India (2018(b))

4.5 Indian AD Cases Against ASEAN-6

India has strategically applied anti-dumping duties against four ASEAN countries aggressively. Although the Philippines and Vietnam have been relatively safer in comparison, they have become the target of India's anti-dumping actions in recent years. Specifically, India has targeted Thailand and Indonesia with the highest number of anti-dumping cases initiated against them, followed by Malaysia in third place, and Singapore at the fourth place. The Indian anti-dumping measures against the ASEAN during the period 1995–2015 elaborate Indian AD policy features. Indian anti-dumping cases target those ASEAN countries which hold the more substantial trade surpluses with India.

Table 4.2 shows that how many of 133 cases initiated against ASEAN countries resulted in final duties and how many did not. In (86%) of cases duties were imposed, and (13%) did not. However, since the initiation of a case itself can influence the value and volume of imports from named countries, these cases are still included in the data for analysis.

Figure 4.2 shows the time trend of India's anti-dumping measures against six ASEAN countries. There is a rising stream of anti-dumping cases against Thailand and Indonesia from the 1995s, while against Singapore and Malaysia comparatively lesser no. of anti-dumping cases. From 1995 to 2000, the anti-dumping cases against ASEAN concentrated on three countries: Indonesia (07) followed by Thailand (06) and Malaysia (03). These three countries accounted for more than 90% share.

While during 2000–2006, this trend shifted towards Singapore (20), Thailand (12), Indonesia (11), and Malaysia (08), respectively, Fig. 4.2. The number of anti-dumping initiations against ASEAN countries increased significantly during 2007–2015 following the global financial crisis in 2008 due to cases against the Philippines (2) and Vietnam (9). During this period India's anti-dumping cases increasingly targeted Thailand (21), Malaysia (16), Indonesia (11), and Singapore (4).

Table 4.2 Summary of AD case against ASEAN-6 imports, Ministry of Commerce and Industry of India (2018(a))

Targeted country	Number of cases initiated	Number of cases with the final duty	Number of cases with no measures
Thailand	39	35	5
Indonesia	29	27	2
Malaysia	27	23	3
Singapore	26	25	1
Vietnam	9	4	5
Philippines	3	1	2
Total	133	115	18
Total percentage share	100	86.46	13.53

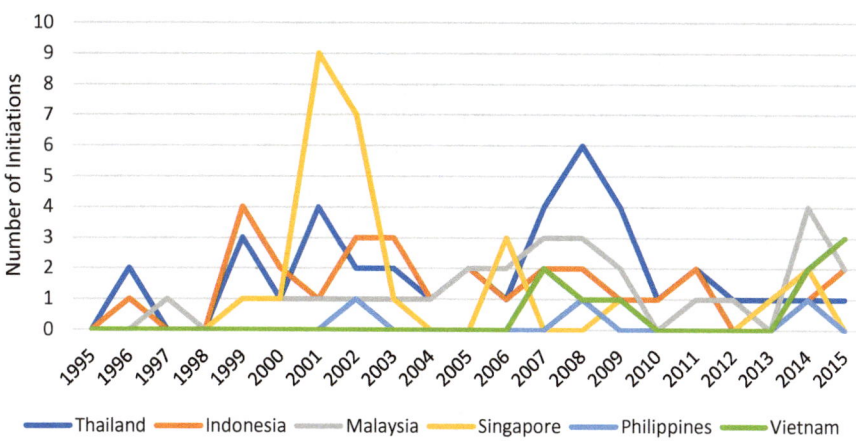

Fig. 4.2 Trend of India's anti-dumping cases against ASEAN 6 imports

Table 4.3 AD case by industries against ASEAN-6 (1995–2015)Ministry of Commerce and Industry of India (2018(a))

Industry	Indonesia	Malaysia	Singapore	Thailand	Philippines	Vietnam	Total (percent of total no of cases)
Chemicals	12	7	17	13	0	0	49(37.1)
Machinery	1	7	2	4	1	4	19(14.3)
Textiles	6	4	0	7	0	1	18(13.6)
Metal	1	3	3	4	2	0	13(0.09)
Plastics	2	2	3	5	0	1	13(0.08)
Wood	2	2	0	1	0	1	06(0.04)
Stones and glasses	3	0	0	2	0	0	05(0.03)
Paper	2	1	0	0	0	0	03(0.02)
Rubber	0	0	1	1	0	0	02(0.01)
Optical	0	1	0	1	0	1	02(0.01)
Electrical	0	0	0	0	0	1	01(0.00)
Transport	0	0	0	1	0	0	01(0.00)
Total	29	27	26	39	03	09	133

During the same period 17 anti-dumping cases are initiated by these countries against India. Indonesia initiated 14 cases, Thailand initiated two cases, and Malaysia launched one case. While no case is initiated by the Philippines, Singapore, and Vietnam leaving no cause for India's retaliation against these countries.

In Table 4.3, I report the pattern of anti-dumping cases initiation by domestic Indian industries against ASEAN-6 imports. Clearly, Chemical industry leads with

(37%) of the initiations, followed by Machinery and Mechanical appliances (19%), textiles (18%), Metals (13%), and Plastics (13%). In fact, out of these 133 cases initiated by India, 84% of cases have been filled by these five industries. This situation is closely related to the current world economic market structure where the Indian industries such as Chemicals, Plastics, and machinery have to compete with ever increasing imported products (Choi and Kim 2014).

Chemical industry initiated the highest no. of cases against Singapore followed by Thailand, Indonesia, and Malaysia. Machinery and mechanical industry launched the highest number of cases against Malaysia followed by Thailand, the Philippines, and Singapore.

Interestingly, More than 50 percent of antidumping cases against Indonesia and Malaysia concentrated in two industries: Chemicals, Machinery and mechanical. For Thailand, (40%) of the cases are from these two industries. While for Singapore, more than (70%) of the cases are from these two industries only. For the Philippines (30%) and Vietnam (50%) of the cases are from these two industries. Bagchi et al. (2015) that reported the direct relationship between the growth of the major manufacturing industry India and filling of anti-dumping cases by the respective industry groups.

4.6   Data

Global Anti-dumping Database of the WTO covers all the Anti-dumping cases initiated by India from 1992 to 2015. Further, Indian AD authority viz. Directorate general of trade remedies analysis on these cases serves to identify the cases outcomes. Imports volume based on International Trade Classification of the Harmonised System at the six-digit classification level has been used from United Nation Comtrade for the period 1995–2015.

4.6.1   Methodology

In order to estimate the trade effect of Anti-dumping measures on imports I specified an empirical model of the form

$$\ln\left(x_i, t_j\right) = \alpha + \beta_0 \ln\left(x_{i,t-1}\right) + \beta_1 \ln\left(x_{i,t-1}\right)/\ln\left(x_{i,-2}\right) + \beta_2 \ln\left(\text{Duty}_i\right) \\ + \beta_3(\text{Num Named}) + \beta_4\left(td_j\right) + \beta_5\left(td_j * \text{dec}_i\right) + \varepsilon_i.$$

The variable $\ln(x_i, t_j)$ denotes the volume of the imported good from named countries at time t_j, where ($j = -2, -1, 0, 1, 2, 3, 4, 5$). $\ln(x_{i, t-1})$ is the volume of the imported good from named countries 1 year before anti-dumping case initiation. The ratio $\ln(x_{i, t-1})/\ln(x_{i, t-2})$ specifies change in the volume of the imported good from named countries one and 2 years before the anti-dumping case initiation. Duty$_i$

denotes the anti-dumping duty on each named country imports volume. Num Named is the dummy variable. It is one if the three or more countries are named in a particular case and zero, otherwise. td_j is a time dummy variable. It is one in the year, ($j = 0$) and zeroes in all other years. Dec is also a dummy variable. Its value is one if duty is positive and zero otherwise.

Similar model is employed to estimate the trade effect of anti-dumping measures for the imports volume from non-named countries which comprises all those countries that are not named in the particular cases (viz. remaining ASEAN and Non-ASEAN) countries. Finally, estimation for all trading countries overall is also estimated.

Each AD case initiated against the ASEAN-6 country's imports for the 20-year period generated panel data. Information on India's AD cases decision regarding affirmative, negative and withdrawn against ASEAN-6 is from Global Anti-dumping Database. Taking the log of the imports volume from named and non-named countries the estimation is performed using pooled OLS. Although it is not a best measure for the estimation but due to the lack of sufficient instruments and endogeneity problem in variables, I have chosen this method Woolridge (2002).

4.7   Empirical Results

Table 4.4 presents the empirical results and I to interpret the coefficients. The first column shows the impact on named ASEAN-6 countries imports in each case. The second column shows the impact on named non-named countries imports. And the

Table 4.4 Results of AD cases against named ASEAN-6 imports vs. not-named ASEAN and other vs. all countries

Variable	Named ASEAN	Non-named (ASEAN and other countries)	All countries
$\ln(x_{i(t-1)})$	$0.0843^{***}(0.033)$	$0.939(0.298)$	$1.005(0.173)$
$\ln$ (% change in x_i $_{(t-1)}/x_{i(t-2)})$	$0.574(0.209)$	$0.887(0.024)$	$-0.951(1.529)$
In (duty)	$-0.0241^{***}(0.050)$	$-0.067^{***}(0.046)$	$-0.085^{***}(0.048)$
No. of countries named	$-0.257^{**}(0.215)$	$0.131^{**}(0.113)$	$0.104^{**}(0.112)$
In duty $\times t_0$	$0.090(0.153)$	$-0.016^{**}(0.067)$	$-0.008^{***}(0.019)$
In duty $\times t_1$	$-0.040^{**}(0.041)$	$-0.012(0.019)$	$0.017^{***}(0.018)$
In duty $\times t_2$	$-0.056(0.039)$	$0.017(0.018)$	$-0.013^{***}(0.018)$
In duty $\times t_3$	$-0.019(0.038)$	$-0.020(0.018)$	$-0.009^{***}(0.018)$
In duty $\times t_4$	$0.057(0.038)$	$-0.015^{*}(0.018)$	$-0.044(0.065)$
Constant	$1.062^{**}(0.287)$	$1.029^{**}(0.305)$	$1.187^{**}(1.645)$
R^2	0.648	0.849	0.851
No. of observations	1511	11,571	15,720

*denotes significance at 1%
**denotes significance at 5%
***denotes significance at 10%

third column shows the impact on overall countries imports due to Indian AD cases initiation on ASEAN imports.

The coefficient for the one-year lagged import volume of imported good before the case initiation is positive and statistically significant (at 1% level) for named ASEAN countries as shown in first row Table 4.4. For non-named countries and overall the coefficient remains positive and insignificant.

The ratio of one- and two-year lagged import volume before the AD case initiation is positive and statistically significant at (5% level) for named ASEAN countries Table 4.4. It implies that (10%) change in the past import volume increases the current import volume by more than (55%) during the investigation period. For non-named countries, this ratio explains large variations in current import volume. For overall countries, the coefficient is negative and insignificant which means a change in past import volume deters the volume of imported good from named and non-named countries.

The coefficient for duty is negative and significant (at 1% level). i.e., (10%) increase in duty cause the imports volume to decline by more than 2% for named ASEAN countries as shown in third row of Table 4.4. For non-named countries, the coefficient is negative and significant (at 1% level), i.e., duty also restricts the trade from the countries not named in the case. For overall countries, the coefficient is negative and significant. Moreover, the degree of impact is higher for non-named and overall countries than named countries.

- The coefficient for the number of countries named is negative and significant as expected (at 5% level) for named ASEAN countries as shown in fourth row of Table 4.4. It implies that opening a case against more than one country deters the imports volume more than the number of the country named is one. On the other hand, for non-named countries and overall the coefficient is positive and significant (at 5% level), i.e., a persistent increase in the volume of imports from the non-named and overall.

- The coefficients of the interactive time dummy and duty in the year 1, 2, and 3 are negative, while the coefficients of the year 0 and 4 are positive for named ASEAN countries as shown in (fifth, sixth, . . ., eighth, ninth) rows of Table 4.4. It implies that the volume of imports from named countries increases during initiation year then it falls continuously during 3 years with duty. The value is significant for the second year at (5% level) and insignificant for all the years. The effect of duty starts fading in the fourth year, and import value increases during the fourth year. For non-named ASEAN, the coefficients of the years ($j = 0,1,3$ and 4) are negative and insignificant except the year ($j = 2$). It implies that although, import volume from countries non-named decreases due to the duties but the decline in volume is insignificant Table 4.4. On comparing the extent of reduction in imports value from named which is (-0.040) and non-named (-0.016) in the year ($j = 1$). It is quite evident that named country imports mostly feel the impact of duties due to a more significant decline in their import volume in comparison to non-named import volume. For overall countries, the coefficients for all the year after the duty are negative and significant at (1% level). It is most significant in the first year which implies that imports volume decreases from named and non-named throughout and suggests the possibility of overall trade depression. From the above analysis, it is evident that duties reduce the trade from named ASEAN countries and non-named countries. However, a positive coefficient for imports volume from non-named countries after duty imposition suggests the possibility of trade diversion from non-named countries imports. The constant term is statistically significant (at 5% level) for the name as well as non-named and insignificant for overall.

4.8 Conclusion

This study examines the efficacy of India's anti-dumping measures on trade flows from six ASEAN countries for the period 1995–2015. To investigate the impact of anti-dumping measures on import volume of six ASEAN countries the autoregressive model is estimated by regressing imports volume for the 5 years on its past two lagged import volume, size of duty, number of countries named in the cases, time and decision dummies. The paper's empirical estimation results reveal that ASEAN countries imports volume declines with the usage of anti-dumping duties, and trade has reduced from the named ASEAN countries with insignificant trade diversion from non-named countries, which indicates that the anti-dumping policy has a substantial investigation effect on their imports. Besides, welfare effects of anti-dumping policy on consumers and the domestic industry have not been examined. It is quite apparent that the anti-dumping policy is successful in restricting imports. Indeed, the study gives positive and significant results of trade depression from overall countries. Findings validate that anti-dumping policy restricts the trade from all the countries other than named ASEAN after a lag of 2 years. Therefore, it can be concluded that the anti-dumping policy depresses the trade for all its trading partners per the previous research results. On the other hand, it is also crucial that FTA between India-ASEAN enacted the lesser duty rules and did not prohibit contracting countries to initiate anti-dumping duty (Article 3(8)) of the ASEAN-INDIA FREE TRADE AGREEMENT. This study points for the alternative policy in the place of anti-dumping duty in for improving the overall trade potential with ASEAN-6 region.

References

Aggarwal, A. (2003). Patterns and determinants of anti-dumping: A worldwide perspective. *ICRIER, Working Paper: 113.*

Aggarwal, A. (2010). Trade effects of anti-dumping in India: Who benefits? *The International Trade Journal, 25*(1), 112–158.

Ahmed, S. (2010). SSRN Electric Journal, https://doi.org/10.2139/ssrn.1698849

Bagchi, S., Bhattacharyya, S., & Narayanan, K. (2015). Anti-dumping initiations in Indian manufacturing industries. *South Asia Economic Journal, 16*(2), 278–294.

Blonigen, B. A., & Prusa, T. J. (2016). Dumping and antidumping duties. In K. Bagwell & R. W. Staiger (Eds.), *Handbook of commercial policy* (Vol. 1, pp. 107–159). North-Holland: Elsevier.

Bown, C. P. (2008). The WTO and antidumping in developing countries. *Economics and Politics, 20*(2), 255–288.

Brenton, P. (2001). Anti-dumping policies in the EU and trade diversion. *European Journal of Political Economy, 17*(3), 593–607.

Choi, C. H., & Kim, J. W. (2014). Determinants for macroeconomic factors of antidumping: A comparative analysis of India and China. *The International Trade Journal, 28*(3), 229–245.

Cuyvers, L., & Dumont, M. (2005). EU anti-dumping measures against ASEAN countries: Impact on trade flows. *Asian Economic Journal, 19*(3), 249–271.

Ganguli, B. (2008). The trade effects of Indian antidumping actions. *Review of International Economics, 16*(5), 930–941.

Kim, H. J., & Kang, M. (2017). Trade diversion effects of anti-dumping duties in selected ASEAN countries. *Journal of International Trade & Commerce, 13*(6), 153–170.

Konings, J., Vandenbussche, H., & Springael, L. (2001). Import diversion under European anti-dumping policy. *Journal of Industry, Competition, and Trade, 1*(3), 283–299.

Mah, J. S. (1999). The United States' antidumping decisions against the ASEAN countries. *ASEAN Economic Bulletin, 16*, 18–27.

Ministry of Commerce and Industry of India. (2018a). *Data on anti-dumping investigations.* Retrieved September 10, 2018, from http://www.dgtr.gov.in/.

Ministry of Commerce and Industry of India. (2018b). *Data on Imports from ASEAN countries.* Retrieved September 20, 2018, from http://commerce-app.gov.in/eidb/icntq.asp.

Ministry of Commerce and Industry of India. (2018c). *Document of Comprehensive Economic Cooperation Agreement between the republic of India and the Association of South East.* Retrieved October 2, 2018, from http://commerce.gov.in/trade/ASEANIndia%20Trade%20in %20Goods%20Agreement.pdf

Moore, M. O., & Zanardi, M. (2009). Does antidumping use contribute to trade liberalization in developing countries? *Canadian Journal of Economics, 42*(2), 469–495.

Park, S. (2009). The trade depressing and trade diversion effects of antidumping actions: The case of China. *China Economic Review, 20*(3), 542–548.

Prusa, T. J. (1996). *The trade effects of US antidumping actions (No. w5440).* National Bureau of Economic Research.

Prusa, T. J. (2001). On the spread and impact of anti-dumping. *Canadian Journal of Economics/ Revue canadienne d'économique, 34*(3), 591–611.

Raju, K. D. (2008). *World Trade Organization agreement on anti-dumping: A GATT/WTO and Indian jurisprudence* (Vol. 15). The Netherlands: Kluwer Law International.

Vandenbussche, H., & Viegelahn, C. (2013). Indian antidumping measures against China: evidence from monthly trade data. Foreign Trade Review.

Viner, J. (1923). *Dumping: A problem in international trade.* Chicago: University of Chicago Press.

World Trade Organization, Anti-Dumping Initiation. (2016). By reporting member vs. exporter 01/01/1995–31/12/2015. Retrieved August 22, 2018, from https://www.wto.org/english/tratop_ e/adp_e/adp_e.htm

Wu, M. (2012). Antidumping in Asia's emerging giants. *Harvard International Law Journal, 53*, 1.

Chapter 5
Examining the Performance of MSME Firm in India: An Empirical Analysis at Industry Level

Abhishek Kumar Sinha ⓘ, Aswini Kumar Mishra ⓘ, and R. L. Manogna

5.1 Introduction

The micro, small and medium enterprises have developed into a very dynamic and productive part of Indian economy since independence. They contribute to creating a very large number of formal and informal employment in our country next only to agriculture. MSMEs produce both producing raw materials and capital goods. They not only create goods and services for retail consumption but also perform the role of ancillary units for large scale Industries. MSMEs create a positive business environment by fostering a spirit of innovation and entrepreneurship among millions of enterprising individuals. MSMEs with outward orientation, produce goods and services for foreign markets, thus providing a valuable exchange of knowledge, both technological and organisational, to our country along with crucial foreign exchange. Small firms act as catalysts for social change and inclusive development creating opportunities of growth for the marginalised classes (MSME 2018).

While MSMEs provide opportunities for growth and employment in India they are constrained due to structural as well as institutional reasons in India. While in developed countries small firms are fountains of innovation, capturing new markets and new niches, in India MSMEs in the manufacturing sector in particular are mainly a source of livelihood competing in markets often with what is termed as frugal innovation or *jugaad* and mostly production products for the local markets and industries.

In this paper we examine the performance of MSME firms at the disaggregated level, where we first consider the performance of 'micro and small firms' (sometimes referred as 'small' firms in this paper) vis-a-vis 'medium' scale firms and then we

A. K. Sinha (✉) · A. K. Mishra · R. L. Manogna
Department of Economics, BITS Pilani, K K Birla Goa Campus, Sancoale, Goa, India
e-mail: aswini@goa.bits-pilani.ac.in

© The Author(s), under exclusive license to Springer Nature Switzerland AG 2021   69
A. K. Mishra et al. (eds.), *Advances in Innovation, Trade and Business*,
Contributions to Management Science,
https://doi.org/10.1007/978-3-030-60354-0_5

examine the performance of firms of different industry classifications. We also look into the antecedents and determinants of firm performance and R&D expenditure at a disaggregate level. The rest of the paper proceeds as follows: In the next section we present, review of literature in context with our study. In Sect. 5.3 we discuss the research gap and our research problem. In Sects. 5.4 and 5.5, we discuss our data and methodology, respectively. In Sect. 5.6 we analyse our empirical results followed by discussions and conclusions in Sect. 5.7.

5.2   Theory and Review of Literature

Neoclassical economists (Solow 1956; Romer 1994) theorise that with diminishing marginal returns to scale, long-run growth can be achieved only through technical progress. So it becomes extremely important to understand the antecedents and determinants of growth and performance of small and medium enterprises (SMEs). It is also important to understand if the growth is happening due to innovation-related activities, since in the long run it is instrumental for the better performance of the economy as a whole (Sinha et. al. 2019). Thus, in this paper, we try to understand if the performance of MSMEs in India is correlated with factors such as research and development activities and outward orientation. We also examine the correlation of firm performance with other structural variables such as firm size which reflects economies of scale, firm age which reflects experience and maturity of firms and capital intensity which shows the extent of involvement of capital in the production process. For measuring firm performance, we can use performance-driven parameters such as the increase in sales, profit, productivity or efficiency. In our study, we analyse the antecedents of firm performance in general first, and then we study the performance of 'micro and small' scale firms vis-a-vis 'medium' scale firms. To allow us to get a better comprehension of underlying issues, we study the theory regarding the influence of structural variables and review the extant literature regarding the relationship. We try to understand these issues with the help of research on innovation and firm growth and performance as a theoretical background.

Firm size is one of the most popular structural variables used by several researchers in trying to explain the performance of firms due to the apparent reasons (Acs and Audretsch 1990; Griffith et al. 2006). The larger firm size provides a formalised structure of the firm and gives them access to financial institutions. They become capable of manoeuvring the political and bureaucratic apparatus of the state for favourable policy-making, and above all larger size provides the economic effects of economies of scale and scope in the overall production process (Seenaiah and Rath 2017). MSMEs suffer from several barriers to growth, such as competition from larger firms and constraints of cash flow to the production process. But they survive against all the odds due to their agility and their innovative practices. They are also bestowed with quick decision-making ability and the ability to make effective changes in response to changes in the business environment. Considering the contrasting effects that firm size has on firm performance and innovative capabilities of firms in general and MSMEs in particular it is important to test the relation of firm size as an explanatory variable for small firm performance.

Another important explanatory variable for the study of firm performance is the effect of firm age (Huergo and Jaumandreu 2004; Majocchi et al. 2005; Fletcher and Harris 2012; D'Angelo et al. 2013). Empirical evidence in this regard from several countries have come to diverse conclusions and hence it becomes pertinent to test the association of firm age with firm performance in the India MSME context. It is important to ask which firms perform better, young firms or mature firms. The literature regarding firm age looks at it from different perspectives. The first obvious perspective is that firm age reflects firm experience and that older firms have better experience in understanding the production process due their learning process. They will also have better understanding of the markets as well as the institutions. They would have better access to credit. The other school of thought links firm age to sclerotic thinking having rigidity and lack of responsiveness (Johanson and Vahlne 1977). It also reflects loss of the ability to adapt for older firms. D'Angelo et al. (2013) describe that firm experience and learning over a period of time may lead to routines and competencies which could be either productive or counterproductive depending on the market conditions prevailing in that sector. In the manufacturing sector firm age could reflect obsolete tools, techniques, machinery and processes which could lead to inefficiencies getting entrenched in the plant. Another important aspect is the risk propensity of manufacturing MSMEs. Young firms undertake efforts that are risky in nature. Older firms in comparison are mature and undertake less risky decisions. Such activities mean higher risks and higher returns for young firms. Thus it is important for our study to examine the age effects on firm performance.

Firm age also reflects managerial flexibility of firms leading to better adjustment to the economic environment of business. The inflexibility or flexibility of organisational routines also determines a firm's organisational learning capability (Leonard-Barton 1992). Acceptance of new knowledge from inside or outside the firm could be negatively related to firm age as managerial processes are developed and organisational routines and rigidities form over a period of time. On the other hand age of firms may denote experience and maturity to understand the market and institutions and help firms in the process of imbibing organisational learning from experience (D'Angelo et al. 2013; Henderson 1999). Thus due to various reasons, the age of firms could be considered an important variable as far as firm performance is concerned.

We need to further analyse the efficiency of the capital utilised by the firm and how that affects the growth and performance for various types of MSMEs in different sectors. Firms that utilise their plant and machinery more efficiently produce higher sales per unit of capital used (Buzzell and Gale 1987). Such firms are said to have higher capital intensity. Thus, capital intensity refers to the ratio of total plant and machinery and other assets used for manufacturing process relative to the output of the firm which has measured in terms of total sales in our study. Thus operating efficiency of plant and machinery employed for generation of goods by manufacturing firms can be captured by its capital intensity .This could also be effective in understanding capacity utilisation by manufacturing MSMEs in India. Kumbhakar et al. (2012) examine the performance of firms in India and results indicate that capital intensity likely to be associated with firm performance for low-tech industries rather than high-tech industries .One has to remember that capital always comes at a cost and due to the cost of capital there could always be a relative decline in the firm performance (deB 1988). It is reasonable to hypothesise that the performance of companies in our sample could well be affected by its capital intensity.

In various studies innovation is defined as any activity, which significantly increases the efficiency and productivity of the firm. According to Teece (2007), R&D activity can be described as a search for new products and process leading to better firm performance. Firm performance is associated with greater competitive advantage which creates prospective above average returns (Crépon et al. 1998). In our study we analyse the correlation and association of firm performance with research and development investment and thus try to understand the role of innovation in performance of firms in Indian MSME context in various sectors of our industry. The results of studies about effects of R&D investment and growth in sales, profitability, efficiency, productivity, etc. remain inconclusive (Cohen and Levinthal 1989; Coe and Helpman 1995; Yang and Chen 2012; Fortune and Shelton 2014). Acs and Audretsch 1990 and Griffith et al. 2006 provide evidence that the MSMEs are as productive and innovative as large firms. Still, we need to be cautious about such conclusions about MSMEs in developing countries. In this context, while Schumpeter himself contends that small firms would effectively challenge large firms due to their innovative capabilities, his later studies show how economies of scale in R&D would lead to scale economies in R&D function itself (Kohn and Scott 2010). One of the critical factors that can influence the R&D performance relationship could be whether they belong to the high technology sector or to the low technology sector since plant and machinery are more important for low technology sectors which for high technology sectors innovation is crucial (Kumbhakar et al. 2012). So, it is essential to determine if in Indian MSMEs what is more important as far as firm performance is considered factors such as capital intensity or R&D. While studies in developed countries have concluded that R&D has a significant impact on the performance of small firms, we need to examine if that relationship holds for Indian MSMEs. Of course, the relative effect of R&D on various sectors of manufacturing MSMEs also needs to be studied.

R&D, in itself, does not impact firm performance. But, R&D leading to innovative product and process followed by effective commercialisation of such new products leads to better firm performance. In the existing literature, the ambiguous nature of R&D-firm performance relationship, especially concerning small firms, compels us to examine the same for our sample under consideration. We consider innovative activities as an important explanatory variable and understand this relationship for Micro, Small and Medium Enterprises, including the impact of R&D expenses on firms of various industry classifications.

It is a considered opinion in developed countries that international trade in general and exports in particular improves the performance of firms. It is argued that exposure to foreign markets improve the learning of the firms involved and results in increase in productivity, better quality of products resulting in growth of sales and profits (Hobday 1995). It is argued that learning from exporting also results in innovative products and processes, which ultimately contributes to better firm performance in the long run. Exporting is considered the starting phase of internationalisation for MSMEs (Leonidou et al. 2010; Wolff and Pett 2000). A firms exposure to export markets lead to improved technological information better machines and tool and moreover firm knowledge which in turn is theorised to improves firm performance (Yeoh 2004). But what is true for firms in developed countries may not apply to firms in developing countries. Firms in developing countries endure various risk factors and unforeseen circumstances when they undertake exporting activities. Involvement of various fixed costs and sunk costs puts undue pressure on firm performance (Westhead et al. 2001). Thus, export could be a risky proposition for firms in developing countries such as India where there is lack of institutional support for small firms and may have serious pitfalls for the financial health of the firms involved in such activities. Another measure of internationalisation of firms is import of raw materials from international markets in order to reduce costs. Import from foreign markets leads to small firms gaining cost advantage over competitor firms in the domestic markets .Thus we need to analyse the impact of import of raw materials as well when we study the effects of internationalisation process and outward orientation of firms and its impact on firm growth.

5.3 Research Gap and Research Problem

There is also a lack of existing research work in the Indian context explaining firm performance for SMEs at behaviour at the disaggregate level and in most studies micro, small and medium enterprises are treated at an aggregate level without considering the heterogeneities in MSMEs of different types. Even when we find such studies they are not studied with sectoral level differences. We intend to investigate determinants of firm performance and the extent to which these factors influence the firm performance at a disaggregate level of 'micro and small' firms vis-a-vis 'medium' scale firms. We also examine the determinants of firm performance at the industry level. An empirical study is required taking into account the hetero-geneous nature of MSMEs at the industry level also.

5.4 Data

In order to explore the factors affecting the performance of Indian manufacturing MSME firms, we consider only manufacturing firms whose plant and machinery are limited to Rupees 100 million from the Centre for Monitoring Indian Economy (CMIE) Prowess database.

According to the classification of the MSME Act, 2006 a "Micro Enterprises" in manufacturing sector is a firm with plant & machinery investment restricted to Rupees 2.5 million; a "Small Enterprise" in manufacturing sector is a firm with plant & machinery investment more than Rupees 2.5 million but not exceeding Rupees 50 million ; while a "Medium Enterprises" in manufacturing sector is a firm with plant & machinery investment larger than Rupees 50 million but restricted to the limit of Rupees 100 million (The Gazette of India, Sep 2006; MSME 2018). Manufacturing MSMEs consistently produce about a third of the Gross Output produced by the Indian Economy (MSME 2018).

We further segregate this list to get a panel of micro, small and medium enterprises operational in 2006 based on the plant and machinery investment as specified by the Government of India—Micro, Small and Medium Enterprises Development (MSMED) Act, 2006. We construct a balanced panel of 720 MSME firms from the firm-level data accessible at CMIE Prowess IQ database for the period of 2006–2017, comprising of 63.3% micro and small firms and 36.7% of medium-scale firms. The resulting sample is a balanced panel data with about 8542 firm-year observations (Figs. 5.1, 5.2, 5.3, 5.4, 5.5, 5.6; Tables 5.1 and 5.2).

Table 5.3 shows the summary statistics for the sample of firms considered in the estimation (Table 5.4).

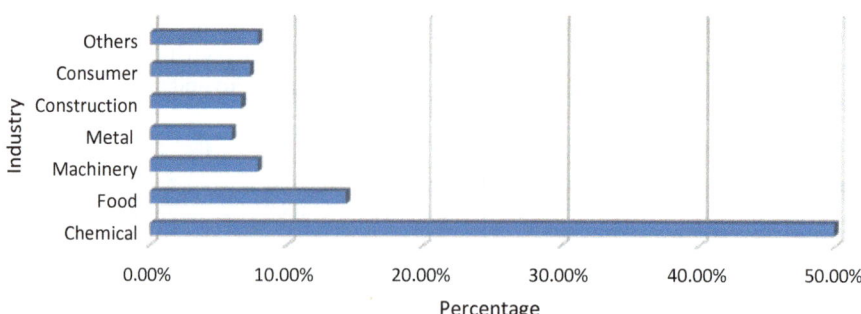

Fig. 5.1 Distribution of sample firms by industry classification

Firm Size and Retutn on Assets (ROA)

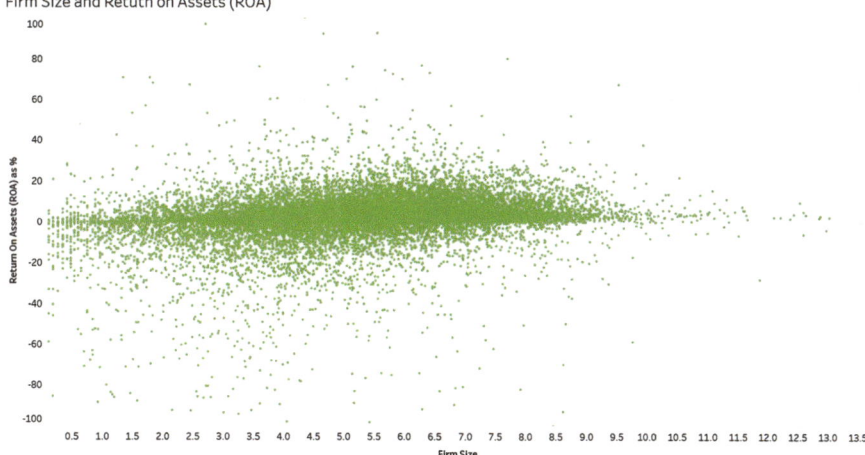

Fig. 5.2 Relationship between firm size and firm performance (ROA)

Firm Age and Retutn on Assets (ROA)

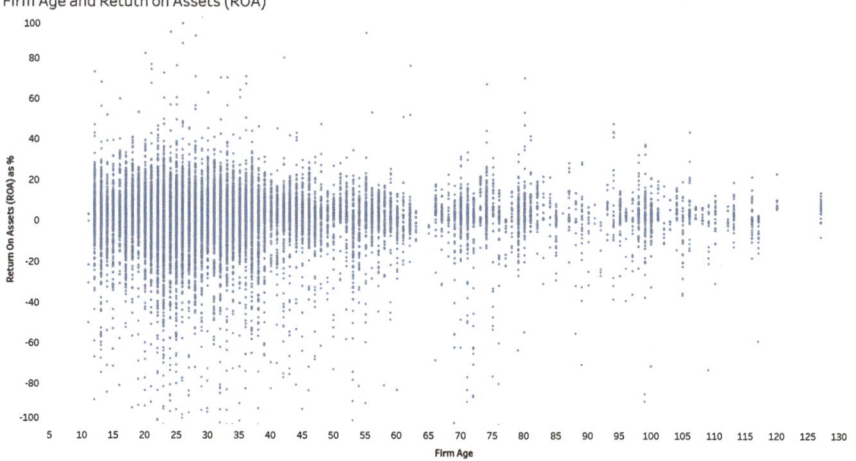

Fig. 5.3 Relationship between firm age and firm performance (ROA)

5.5 Methodology

The fixed effects model assumes that these firm-specific unobserved heterogeneities λ_i are correlated with time-invariant firm-specific unobserved variables (De and Nagaraj 2014).

The dependent variable in this analysis is ROA of a firm 'i' in year 't'. The ROA is a commonly accepted measure of firm performance. The model employed to explain the variation in the firm-level ROA is defined as below:

Model

Capital Intensity and Return on Assets (ROA)

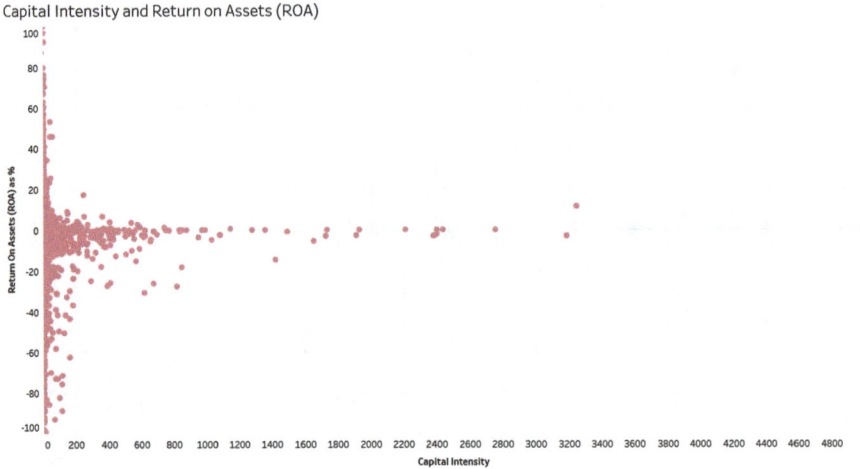

Fig. 5.4 Relationship between capital intensity and firm performance (ROA)

R&D Intensity and Return on Assets (ROA)

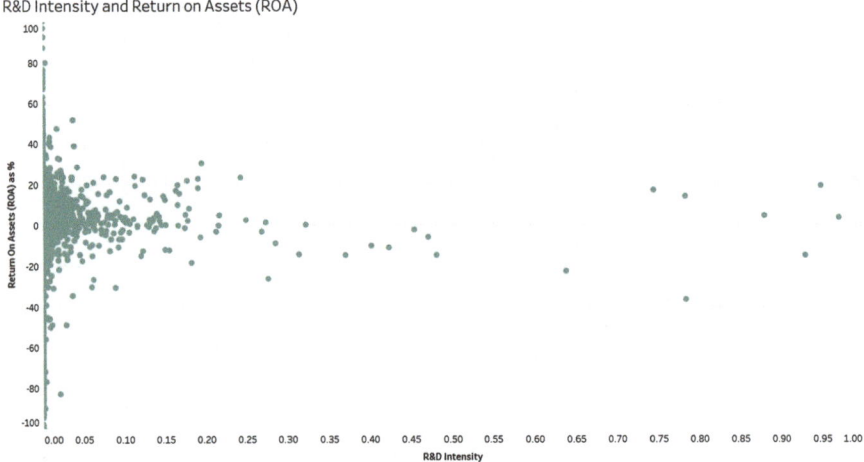

Fig. 5.5 Relationship between R&D Intensity and firm performance (ROA)

$$
\begin{aligned}
\text{ROA}_{it} = {} & \beta_0 + \beta_1 * D_1 * D_2 * \text{Age}_{it} + \beta_2 * D_1 * D_2 * \text{Age}^2{}_{it} + \beta_3 * D_1 * D_2 \\
& * \text{FirmSize}_{it} + \beta_4 * D_1 * D_2 * \text{ExportIntensity}_{it} + \beta_5 * *D_1 * D_2 \\
& * \text{RMII}_{it} + \beta_6 * *D_1 * D_2 * \text{RNDIntensity}_{it} + \beta_7 * *D_1 * D_2 \\
& * \text{CapitalIntensity}_{it} + \varepsilon_{it} \ldots.
\end{aligned}
\tag{5.1}
$$

$D_1 = 1$ "Micro & Small Scale Enterprises" Dummy; $D_1 = 2$ for Medium Scale Enterprises Dummy.

$D_2 = 1$ for Chemical Industry Dummy; $D_2 = 2$ for Food Industry Dummy; $D_2 = 3$ for Machinery Industry Dummy; $D_2 = 4$ for Metal Dummy; $D_2 = 5$ for

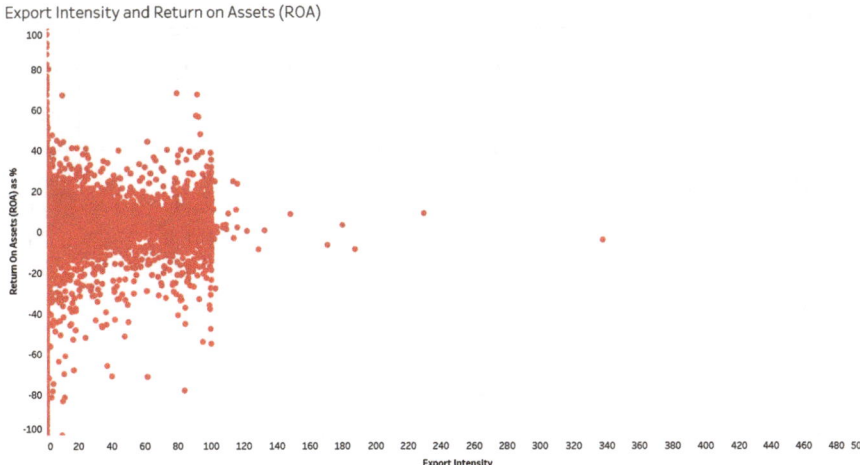

Fig. 5.6 Relationship between export Intensity and firm performance (ROA)

Table 5.1 Definition of variables

Variable	Type	Description
Dependent variable		
ROA	%	Return on assets (measure of firm performance)
Explanatory variables		
Firm age	Continuous	Current year—year of incorporation
Firm age squared	Continuous	Square of firm age (captures non-linear effects of firm age)
Firm size	Continuous	Firm size measured as sales /logarithm of sales
Export intensity	%	The ratio of export/sales (export/sales)
Raw material import intensity	%	Raw material imports/raw material purchases
R&D intensity	%	Research and development expense/sales
Capital intensity	%	Total assets/sales

Source: Calculated by authors based on CMIE Prowess data

Table 5.2 Distribution of sample firms by industry classification

S. No.	Industry classification	Percentage
1	Chemical	49.9%
2	Food	14.3%
3	Machinery	7.9%
4	Metal	6.0%
5	Construction	6.7%
6	Consumer	7.3%
7	Others	7.9%

Source: Calculated by authors based on CMIE Prowess data

Table 5.3 Descriptive statistics of the variables

Variable	Obs	Mean	Std. dev.	Min	Max
Firm age	8520	37.9	17.7	12.0	138.0
Export intensity	8532	14.5	34.6	0.0	1819.6
Firm size (sales)	8273	1741.3	12967.6	−66.0	449460.7
RM import intensity	8407	13.0	98.3	0.0	6866.7
R&D intensity	8257	0.0	0.1	−2.3	3.1
Capital intensity	8257	8.0	534.7	−15874.0	38020.7
Return on assets	8453	2.4	11.6	−192.8	90.8

Source: Calculated by authors based on CMIE Prowess data

Table 5.4 Correlations matrix

Variable	Firm size	Export Intensity	RD intensity	Firm age	Firm age squared	Capital intensity	RM import intensity
Firm size	1						
Export intensity	0.0368	1					
RD intensity	−0.0045	0.0127	1				
Firm age	−0.0232	−0.06	−0.0295	1			
Firm age squared	−0.0207	−0.0618	−0.0211	0.9644	1		
Capital intensity	−0.0019	−0.0045	0.0044	−0.0161	−0.0126	1	
RM import intensity	0.0158	0.0399	0.0021	−0.0128	−0.0166	0.0007	1

Source: Calculated by authors based on CMIE Prowess data

Construction Dummy; $D_2 = 6$ for Consumer Industry Dummy; $D_2 = 7$ for Others Industry Dummy.

5.6 Empirical Results

Table 5.5 represents the parameter estimates of the model where we hypothesise that firm performance is determined by the size of the firm, age of the firm, export intensity, raw material import intensity, R&D intensity, and its capital intensity.

The coefficient of the firm size represented by the log of net sales is positive and significant for both Medium firms as well as Small firms at the aggregate level. Thus, economies of scale are confirmed in Indian manufacturing MSME firms. It means that firms with larger size perform better than their smaller counterparts which could be due to various reasons such as their access to financial institutions, higher bargaining power with labour as well as with suppliers, better brand perception as well as reach with government and bureaucratic setup. The coefficient of age is

Table 5.5 Fixed effects for firm performance

Variables		FE Coefficients
Firm size		
Ln net sales—micro & small		3.203^{***}
Ln net sales—medium		4.399^{***}
Export intensity		
Exports to sales—micro & Small		-0.005
Exports to sales—medium		0.009
Raw material import intensity		
RMI to RMP—micro & small		0.003^{***}
RMI to RMP—medium		-0.011^{*}
R & D intensity		
RD intensity—micro & small		-2.659
RD intensity—medium		4.378
Age of firms		
Age—micro & small		-0.638^{***}
Age—medium		-0.844^{***}
Age squared		
AGE2—micro & small		-0.001
AGE2—medium		0.001
Capital intensity		
Capital Intensity—micro & small		0.001^{***}
Capital Intensity—medium		0.004^{***}

Standard errors in parentheses $^{***}p < 0.01$, $^{**}p < 0.05$, $^{*}p < 0.1$
Source: Calculated by authors based on CMIE Prowess data

negative and statistically significant for small firms indicating the Liability of ageing. The problem with Indian manufacturing SMEs is the existence of legacy machines and tools which the older MSMEs are not ready or are incapable of replacing with cutting edge tools and machinery. This is due to several factors such as getting habituated with earlier machines or lack of financial support to go for cutting edge and state-of-the-art tools which can lead to adverse impact on their sales and profitability. The coefficient of R&D intensity and Exports was not found to be significant for MSME firm performance at the aggregate level. R&D activities should lead to new product and process for small firms leading to intellectual property rights and exclusive ability to appropriate such innovations. Severe problems exist with Indian Intellectual Property rights institutions, and it is almost impossible for small firms to enforce their intellectual property rights in the market and protect them from copying and imitation. Since they are not able to appropriate the benefits of their research and development activities, hence it does not reflect in their performance.

Unlike the recent empirical evidence in advanced countries, our estimates of the export intensity do not surface as statistically significant. As far as exports are concerned, we need to understand that they are high risk and high return proposition for firms of even larger size. While large firms can mitigate risks, our study shows that MSME firms in India cannot profit from their exporting activities. The analysis at sectoral levels reflects a similar trend where internationalisation efforts result in non-significant or adverse outcomes as far as firm performance is concerned. According to previous research, 'Raw Material Import Intensity' positively affects firm performance of SMEs (Sinha et al. 2020). Our study shows a similar effect for the micro and small firms since it probably allows them to develop finished products at lower costs. We find no such effect of Raw Material Import Intensity for Medium-scale firms.

The Capital Intensity has a positive and significant effect on firm performance of medium-scale firms indicating the efficiency of capital over labour-intensive MSME firms in India. The same is true for our analysis at a disaggregated level as well as a sectoral level which shows the need for greater investment in modern plant and machinery in the Indian manufacturing sector (Table 5.6).

5.7   Conclusions and Discussions

In our paper, we construct a balanced panel of 720 MSME firms, which have plant and machinery data populated across all the financial years under our consideration, from the firm-level data accessible at CMIE Prowess IQ database for the period of 2006–2017. These firms were segregated as 'Micro and Small' and 'Medium' enterprises based on their investment in plant and machinery. We conducted our analysis at the aggregate level as well as the industry level. Results, at the aggregate level, show that firm performance is significantly influenced by variations in firm size, firm age, raw material import intensity and capital intensity of firms'. At the aggregate level, export intensity and R&D intensity are not found to significantly influence variations in firm performance

Analysis at the disaggregate level found firm performance to be either insignificantly or negatively associated with R&D investment for micro and small firms (e.g. chemical, construction and consumer industry), providing a good rationale for why small firms in India are not R&D intensive. Export intensity is also not found to have a significant affect even at the industry level for any industry category.

The most important implication of our results is that while size, firm age, capital intensity, and raw material import intensity are found to significantly improve firm performance R&D investments and export intensity and are not found to significantly influence firm performance. This is a matter of serious concern for policy makers. Thus, policymakers should foster the spirit of innovation and outward orientation in MSME firms through policy incentives. Indeed, a comprehensive policy for promotion of innovation and exports by small firms is required for the Indian economy.

Table 5.6 Fixed effects model for ROA with industry grouping

Industry group														
	Chemical		Food		Machinery		Metal		Construction		Consumer		Others	
Variables	Mi&S	Med	Mi&S	Med	Mi&S	Med	Mi&S	Med	Mi&S	Med	Mi&S	Med	Mi&S	Med
Firm size	4.77***	3.94***	2.71***	5.75***	9.49***	12.04***	3.55***	0.96	3.22***	10.15***	1.06**	5.94***	1.81**	4.57***
Export intensity	−0.02	−0.02**	−0.04*	−0.04	0	−0.08	0	−0.1	0.02	−0.14	0.01	−0.03	−0.03	0.01
RM import intensity	0.00*	−0.03**	−0.01	0	−0.03	0.08	−0.13**	0.11	−0.04	0.15	0	−0.01	0.06	0
R&D intensity	−4.03*	4.81	78.59	30.5	−0.06	−240.52	−10295.26	19923.22	−62.56**	0	−37.16*	−159.73	−356.36	−169.89
Firm age	−0.72***	−0.73***	−0.59***	−1.16***	−0.78***	−2.05***	−0.90**	0.9	−1.28***	−1.08	−0.43*	−1.40**	−0.59	−1.01*
Firm age squared	0	0	0	0	−0.01*	0.01*	0	−0.02*	0.00*	−0.01	0	0.01	0	0
Capital intensity	0.08***	0.00***	0.01	0.04**	0.16***	3.03***	0.00**	−4.29**	0.01**	0.36***	0	0.01**	0.01	0.02

Standard errors in parentheses *** $p < 0.01$, ** $p < 0.05$, * $p < 0.1$

Source: Calculated by authors based on CMIE prowess data

References

Acs, Z. J., & Audretsch, D. B. (1990). *Innovation and small firms*. Mit Press.

Buzzell, R. D., & Gale, B. T. (1987). *The PIMS principles: Linking strategy to performance*. New York: Simon and Schuster.

Coe, D. T., & Helpman, E. (1995). International R&D spillovers. *European Economic Review, 39* (5), 859–887.

Cohen, W. M., & Levinthal, D. A. (1989). Innovation and learning: The two faces of R & D. *The Economic Journal, 99*(397), 569–596.

Crépon, B., Duguet, E., & Mairessec, J. (1998). Research, innovation and productivity: An econometric analysis at the firm level. *Economics of Innovation and New Technology, 7*(2), 115–158.

D'Angelo, A., Majocchi, A., Zucchella, A., & Buck, T. (2013). Geographical pathways for SME internationalisation: Insights from an Italian sample. *International Marketing Review, 30*(2), 80–105.

De, P. K., & Nagaraj, P. (2014). Productivity and firm size in India. *Small Business Economics, 42* (4), 891–907.

deB, F. H. (1988). Capital intensity and the firm's cost of capital. *The Review of Economics and Statistics*, 587–594.

Fletcher, M., & Harris, S. (2012). Knowledge acquisition for the internationalisation of the smaller firm: Content and sources. *International Business Review, 21*(4), 631–647.

Fortune, A., & Shelton, L. M. (2014). Age matters: Disentangling the effect of R&D investment in the global chemical products industry. *Business Management Dynamics, 3*(11), 35.

Griffith, R., Huergo, E., Mairesse, J., & Peters, B. (2006). Innovation and productivity across four European countries. *Oxford Review of Economic Policy, 22*(4), 483–498.

Henderson, A. D. (1999). Firm strategy and age dependence: A contingent view of the liabilities of newness, adolescence, and obsolescence. *Administrative Science Quarterly, 44*(2), 281–314.

Hobday, M. (1995). Innovation in east Asia: Diversity and development. *Technovation, 15*(2), 55–63.

Huergo, E., & Jaumandreu, J. (2004). How does probability of innovation change with firm age? *Small Business Economics, 22*(3–4), 193–207.

Johanson, J., & Vahlne, J. E. (1977). The internationalisation process of the firm—A model of knowledge development and increasing foreign market commitments. *Journal of International Business Studies, 8*(1), 23–32.

Kohn, M. and Scott J. T. (2010). Source, scale economics in research and development: The Schumpeterian hypothesis. Journal of Industrial Economics, 30(3), 239-249, M

Kumbhakar, S. C., Ortega-Argilés, R., Potters, L., Vivarelli, M., & Voigt, P. (2012). Corporate R&D and firm efficiency: Evidence from Europe's top R&D investors. *Journal of Productivity Analysis, 37*(2), 125–140.

Leonard-Barton, D. (1992). Core capabilities and core rigidities: A paradox in managing new product development. *Strategic Management Journal, 13*(S1), 111–125.

Leonidou, L. C., Katsikeas, C. S., & Coudounaris, D. N. (2010). Five decades of business research into exporting: A bibliographic analysis. *Journal of International Management, 16*(1), 78–91.

Majocchi, A., Bacchiocchi, E., & Mayrhofer, U. (2005). Firm size, business experience and export intensity in SMEs: A longitudinal approach to complex relationships. *International Business Review, 14*(6), 719–738.

MSME. (2018). *Ministry of micro, small and medium enterprises, Government of India*, Annual Report 2017–18.

Romer, P. M. (1994). The origins of endogenous growth. *Journal of Economic Perspectives, 8*(1), 3–22.

Seenaiah, K., & Rath, B. N. (2017). Obstacles to innovation in selected Indian manufacturing firms. *International Journal of Technological Learning, Innovation and Development (IJTLID), 9*(4), 379–398.

Sinha, A. K., Mishra A. K., & Patel, Y. (2019). Firm size, R&D expenditure, and international orientation: an empirical analysis of performance of Indian firms. *International Journal of Technological Learning, Innovation and Development, 11*(4), 311–336

Sinha, A.K, Mishra, A.K., Manogna, R.L., & Prabhudesai R. (2020). Determinants of sustainable financial and innovation performance: A panel data analysis of indian manufacturing SMEs. *International Journal of Business and Globalisation.* In Press.

Solow, R. M. (1956). A contribution to the theory of economic growth. *The Quarterly Journal of Economics, 70*(1), 65–94.

Teece, D. J. (2007). Explicating dynamic capabilities: The nature and microfoundations of (sustainable) enterprise performance. *Strategic Management Journal, 28*(13), 1319–1350.

The Gazette of India. (2006). Government of India.

Yang, C. H., & Chen, Y. H. (2012). R&D, productivity, and exports: Plant-level evidence from Indonesia. *Economic Modelling, 29*(2), 208–216.

Westhead, P., Wright, M., & Ucbasaran, D. (2001). The internationalization of new and small firms: A resource-based view. *Journal of Business Venturing, 16*(4), 333–358.

Wolff, J. A., & Pett, T. L. (2000). Internationalization of small firms: An examination of export competitive patterns, firm size, and export performance. *Journal of Small Business Management, 38*(2), pp. 34–47.

Yeoh, P. (2004). International learning: antecedents and performance implications among newly internationalizing companies in an exporting context. *International Marketing Review, 21*(4/5), 511–535.

Chapter 6
Does Population Ageing Reduce FDI Inflows in OECD Countries? Evidence from Bayesian Panel VAR Estimates

Rajarshi Mitra and Maria Evgenievna Guseva

6.1 Introduction

The importance of foreign direct investment (FDI) for achieving sustainable economic growth is well documented in the existing literature. Both developed and developing economies strive to implement FDI-oriented policies with a view to not only increase foreign capital inflows but also increase the share of FDI inflows in gross domestic product. The OECD countries have been experiencing a decline in population in recent times; in other words, the number of individuals aged 65 and above as a percentage of (a) working population and (b) total population have been steadily increasing. Economic theory argues that there is a negative relationship between population ageing and net FDI inflows. Capital will flow from the industrialized countries with high age-dependency ratios for the old to the "younger" emerging economies that offer relatively higher rates of return on investments. The reasons for population ageing could be attributed to decreases in fertility rates and increases in life expectancies (Narciso 2010). As for the negative effect of population ageing on FDI inflows, the reasons could be country-specific. For instance, Donaldson et al. (2018) argued that the implementation of the one-child policy raised the capital–labour ratio in China and reduced the need for FDI in China.

According to the most recent data released by the World Bank, Japan ranked number one amongst all OECD countries in 2018 with the dependency ratio for the old at 46%, followed by Italy at 36% and Finland at 35%. With the exception of

R. Mitra (✉)
Institute for International Strategy, Tokyo International University, Tokyo, Japan
e-mail: rmitra@tiu.ac.jp

M. E. Guseva
Business Analytical Department, Central Bank of Russian Federation, Moscow, Russian Federation

© The Author(s), under exclusive license to Springer Nature Switzerland AG 2021
A. K. Mishra et al. (eds.), *Advances in Innovation, Trade and Business*,
Contributions to Management Science,
https://doi.org/10.1007/978-3-030-60354-0_6

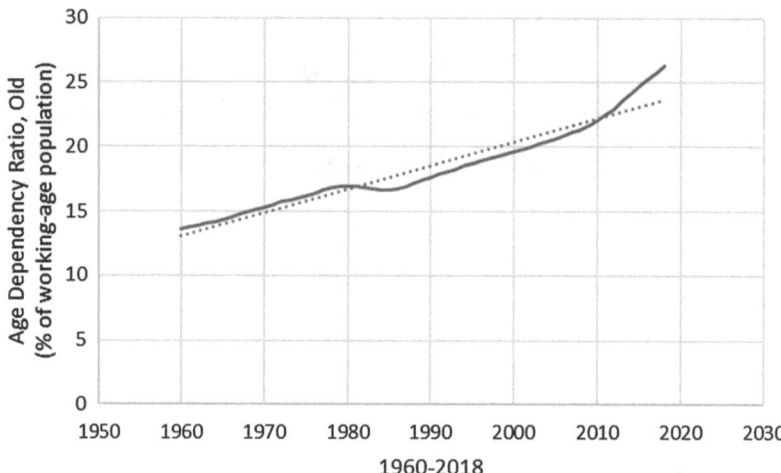

Fig. 6.1 Age-dependency ratio for the old in OECD (*Source:* World Development Indicators, World Bank Group)

Luxembourg, from 1960 until 2018, other OECD members exhibit an overall steady increase in the age-dependency ratio for the old. Figure 6.1 illustrates that the age-dependency ratio for the old, which is the number of individuals aged 65 years and above (% of working age population), has increased sharply in OECD countries over the last 60 years or so.

Will an increase in population ageing lead to a decrease in FDI inflows in OECD countries? Population ageing is viewed as a major concern for the policy makers because of rising social expenditures for the national governments, declines in economic growth, national saving-rates, national investment-rates and tax revenues for the governments. As working age population shrinks, expenditures by the national governments on healthcare for the elderly are expected to rise while tax revenues are expected to fall, thereby raising the possibility of an increase in government budget deficit. A decrease in FDI inflows will have strong implications for the labour market in OECD countries, such as an increase in the unemployment rate.

Although economic theory postulates a link between population ageing and FDI inflows, very few empirical studies have actually investigated the direct relationship between the two variables. In existing studies, the results differ depending on the econometric methodologies and sample periods under consideration, amongst other factors, thereby indicating lack of a general consensus on the significance and the direction of impact of population ageing on FDI inflows. In this paper we estimate a Bayesian panel vector autoregressive model and fill the gap in the existing literature by examining the effects of an increase in population ageing on FDI inflows (as a percentage of GDP) for a panel of 22 OECD countries for the most recent period 1980–2017.

6.2   Literature Review

Two major studies in this field are the life-cycle hypothesis developed by Modigliani and Brumberg (1954), Ando and Modigliani (1963), and the overlapping generations model. In what is considered one of the earliest studies on the relation between population ageing and cross border capital flows, Vernon (1966) argued that, if the number of retired people in total population increases, then the producers will search for markets that offer both lower production costs and higher consumption; thus there will be capital outflow from the country experiencing a declining population. Knickerbocker (1973) cited oligopolistic reason for an increase in FDI inflows to "younger" economies. Narciso (2010) examined the relationship between population ageing and FDI inflows, and also between population ageing and foreign portfolio inflows for 8 capital source countries and 38 capital host countries. Although the author observed a negative effect of old age-dependency ratio on FDI inflows, the period of study was restricted to 2001–2007. Donaldson et al. (2018) showed that demographic changes play an important role in FDI transitions. The one-child policy affected "relative FDI inflows into China versus India, in favor of India".

In a recent discussion paper, Mitra and Abedin (2020) studied the short-run and long-run effects of population ageing on FDI inflows (in proportion to GDP) for Japan, based on ARDL approach to cointegration analysis. Although the short-run effects were found to be insignificant, a significantly positive association between the variables was observed in the long run. The positive long-run effect was a contradiction to the predictions of economic theory. Thus, regardless of the direction of impact of increases in population ageing on FDI inflows (positive or negative), existing literature reveals a significant link between population ageing and FDI inflows in both developed and developing economies.

6.3   Data and the Model

6.3.1   Data

We use annual time series data on 22 OECD countries from the World Development Indicators of the World Bank Group. The countries in our study are Australia, Austria, Canada, Chile, Denmark, Finland, France, Germany, Iceland, Ireland, Israel, Italy, Japan, Mexico, Netherlands, New Zealand, Norway, Portugal, Spain, Sweden, the U.K. and the USA. The sample period is 1980–2017. The dependent variable is net FDI inflows (as a percentage of GDP). The variable is indexed *FDI* in our model. We use two different measures for population ageing as an explanatory variable: (a) age-dependency ratio for the old, which is the number of individuals aged 65 and above as a percentage of working age population, and (b) the number of individuals aged 65 and above as a percentage of total population. The two variables are indexed in the model as *DRO* and *OLD*, respectively. Working age population includes individuals aged between 15 and 64 years. The control variables are (a) trade openness, which is measured as the sum of exports and imports as a percentage of GDP, (b) domestic investment as a percentage of GDP and (c) the real effective exchange rate index with 2010 as the base year. In our model, trade-to-GDP ratio is indexed *OPN*, domestic investment (as a percentage of GDP) is indexed *INV*, and the real effective exchange rate index is denoted as *RER*.

6.3.2 The Model

Apart from using two different measures of population ageing, we test two bivariate models and two multivariate models. In bivariate model 1, we examine the effect of population ageing on the net FDI inflows (as a percentage of GDP), where population ageing is measured by an increase in the number of individuals aged 65 and above as a percentage of working age population. In bivariate model 2, we examine the effect of population ageing on the net FDI inflows (as a percentage of GDP), where population ageing is measured by an increase in the number of individuals aged 65 and above as a percentage of total population. Multivariate model 1 and model 2 are variations of the bivariate models, to the extent that we control for trade openness, domestic investment (as a percentage of GDP) and the real effective exchange rate index. Following Mitra and Abedin (2020), we estimate the following VAR model specifications.

Bivariate model 1:

$$FDI_t = \alpha_1 + \sum_{l=i}^{p} \theta_{1i}FDI_{t-i} + \sum_{l=i}^{p} \theta_{2i}DRO_{t-i} + \varepsilon_t \tag{6.1}$$

Bivariate model 2:

$$FDI_t = \alpha_2 + \sum_{i=1}^{m} \theta_{1i}FDI_{t-i} + \sum_{i=0}^{p} \theta_{2i}OLD_{t-i} + \mu_t \tag{6.2}$$

Multivariate model 1:

$$FDI_t = \alpha_3 + \sum_{i=1}^{m} \theta_{1i}FDI_{t-i} + \sum_{i=0}^{p} \theta_{2i}DRO_{t-i} + \sum_{l=i}^{p} \theta_{3i}OPN_{t-i} +$$

$$\sum_{l=i}^{p} \theta_{4i}INV_{t-i} + \sum_{l=i}^{p} \theta_{5i}RER_{t-i} + \vartheta_t \tag{6.3}$$

Multivariate model 2:

$$\text{FDI}_t = \alpha_4 + \sum_{i=1}^{m} \theta_{1i}\text{FDI}_{t-i} + \sum_{i=0}^{p} \theta_{2i}\text{OLD}_{t-i} + \sum_{l=i}^{p} \theta_{3i}\text{OPN}_{t-i}$$

$$+ \sum_{l=i}^{p} \theta_{4i}\text{INV}_{t-i} + \sum_{l=i}^{p} \theta_{5i}\text{RER}_{t-i} + \gamma_t \qquad (6.4)$$

6.3.3   Estimation Method

We perform four panel unit root tests, namely, Levin et al. (2002), Im et al. (2003), Fisher-ADF and Fisher-PP tests defined by Maddala and Wu (1999) and Choi (2001). If the variables are found to be either stationary or I(1) with *no* cointegration, then we estimate a Bayesian panel VAR model. We also estimate IRFs to examine the response of FDI (as a percentage of GDP) to shocks to each of the two different measures of population ageing. For completeness, we report the coefficient estimates for every VAR model; however, in our discussion of the main results, we focus on the FDI equation, which is the equation of interest in our study.

6.4   Main Results

6.4.1   Panel Unit Root Tests

The results of the panel unit root tests, performed with (a) constant only (Case I) and (b) constant with trend (Case II), at levels and first-differences, are reported in Table 6.1. The null hypothesis of a unit root is tested against the alternative of no unit root. The results, overall, indicate that all six panel variables are stationary.

The results for both Case I and Case II indicate that the variable FDI is stationary. The variable OPN is found to be stationary in Case II. The variable INV is found to be stationary in both Case I and Case II. The variable RER is found to be stationary in both Case I and Case II. The ADF-Fisher test in Case I and the LLC test in Case II show that the variable DRO is stationary. The LLC, IPS and ADF-Fisher tests in Case II show that the variable OLD is stationary. Since the variables, overall, are found to be stationary, we estimate a Bayesian panel VAR model. The coefficient estimates for the bivariate

Bayesian panel VAR model are reported in Table 6.2.

The results in column (2) in Table 6.2 indicate that an increase in net FDI inflows (as a percentage of GDP) in the previous 2 years, FDI (−1) and FDI (−2), have significantly positive effects on the net FDI inflows (as a percentage of GDP) at time *t*. The coefficients are significant at the 5% significance level. Increases in the dependency ratio for the old (as a percentage of working age population) and the

Table 6.1 Panel unit root tests

Variable	LLC	IPS	ADF-Fisher	PP-Fisher
Case I: constant only				
FDI	−4.10(0.00)***	−4.69(0.00)***	89.53(0.00)***	206.71(0.00)***
ΔFDI	−12.93(0.00)***	−21.16(0.00)***	438.99(0.00)***	666.62(0.00)***
OPN	−0.09(0.46)	2.12(0.98)	31.64(0.92)	27.57(0.98)
ΔOPN	17.74(0.00)***	−16.78(0.00)***	337.31(0.00)***	524.07(0.00)***
INV	−4.41(0.00)***	−5.78(0.00)***	109.58(0.00)***	61.73(0.04)**
ΔINV	−13.75(0.00)***	−13.27(0.00)***	256.66(0.00)***	301.52(0.00)***
RER	−5.53(0.00)***	−5.47(0.00)***	110.60(0.00)***	62.34(0.04)**
ΔRER	−12.28(0.00)***	−14.95(0.00)***	293.87(0.00)***	414.80(0.00)***
DRO	1.59(0.94)	2.70(0.99)	63.56(0.03)**	1.42(1.00)
ΔDRO	−3.93(0.00)***	−1.88(0.03)**	80.96(0.00)***	16.44(1.00)
OLD	2.19(0.99)	4.91(1.00)	40.90(0.61)	1.69(1.00)
ΔOLD	−3.46(0.00)***	2.05(0.02)**	80.80(0.00)***	19.19(0.99)
Case II: constant and trend				
FDI	−3.30(0.00)***	−4.81(0.00)***	100.33(0.00)***	237.33(0.00)***
ΔFDI	−9.25(0.00)***	−18.83(0.00)***	358.89(0.00)***	3635.62(0.00)***
OPN	−4.05(0.00)***	−2.62(0.00)***	68.34(0.01)**	41.79(0.57)
ΔOPN	−16.10(0.00)***	−14.68(0.00)***	269.35(0.00)***	785.79(0.00)***
INV	−4.04(0.00)***	−5.36(0.00)***	104.92(0.00)***	55.35(0.12)
ΔINV	−11.90(0.00)***	−10.48(0.00)***	187.74(0.00)***	262.39(0.00)***
RER	−4.07(0.00)***	−4.43(0.00)***	92.49(0.00)***	44.22(0.46)
ΔRER	−9.84(0.00)***	−12.48(0.00)***	225.74(0.00)***	409.24(0.00)***
DRO	−11.55(0.00)***	−11.05(0.00)***	240.73(0.00)***	23.41(0.99)
ΔDRO	−2.22(0.01)**	−0.33(0.37)	55.34(0.12)	10.86(1.00)
OLD	−11.39(0.00)***	−10.30(0.00)***	−10.30(0.00)***	16.99(0.99)
Δold	−2.23(0.01)**	0.10(0.54)	50.13(0.24)	10.67(1.00)

The values in parenthesis represent *P*-values
*** Indicates significant at the 1% significance level; ** indicates significant at the 5% significance level

number of individuals aged 65 and above (as a percentage of total population) have insignificant effects on the net FDI inflows (as a percentage of GDP). As per the estimates of the two bivariate models, population ageing does not significantly affect net FDI inflows (as a percentage of GDP). The coefficients for the multivariate Bayesian panel VAR model are reported in Table 6.3.

In multivariate model 1 and model 2, the coefficient estimates for the FDI equation, reported in column (2) in Table 6.3, indicate that an increase in net FDI inflows (as a percentage of GDP) in the previous 2 years, FDI (−1) and FDI (−2), have significantly positive effects on the net FDI inflows (as a percentage of GDP) at time *t*. The coefficients are significant at the 5% significance level. Similar to the estimates of the bivariate models, we find insignificant effects of increases in (a) dependency ratio for the old (as a percentage of working age population), and (b) the number of individuals aged 65 and above (as a percentage of total population)

Table 6.2 Bivariate Bayesian panel VAR estimates

	(2)	(3)
Model 1	FDI	DRO
FDI (−1)	0.53(0.03)**	0.0005(0.0005)
FDI (−2)	0.15(0.03)**	0.0003(0.0004)
DRO (−1)	−0.23(0.62)	1.94(0.01)**
DRO (−2)	0.21(0.64)	−0.94(0.01)**
Constant	1.57(0.72)**	0.02(0.01)
	(2)	(3)
Model 2	FDI	OLD
FDI (−1)	0.53(0.03)**	0.0003(0.0003)
FDI (−2)	0.15(0.03)**	0.0001(0.0002)
OLD (−1)	−0.87(1.16)	1.93(0.01)**
OLD (−2)	0.84(1.18)	−0.93(0.01)**
Constant	1.63(0.69)**	0.01(0.01)**

The values in parenthesis represent standard errors
** Indicates significant at the 5% level

on the net FDI inflows (as a percentage of GDP). Therefore, the multivariate models also indicate that population ageing has no significant effect on net FDI inflows (in proportion to GDP). Furthermore, an increase in trade openness in the previous year, OPN (−1), has a significantly positive effect on net FDI inflows (as a percentage of GDP) at time t. Thus an increase in economic integration, reflected by a higher trade-to-GDP ratio, is expected to increase foreign capital inflows into the 22 OECD countries under study.

Furthermore, Figs. 6.2 and 6.3 indicate that shocks to DRO (age-dependency ratio for the old as a percentage of the working age population) and OLD (the number of individuals aged 65 and above as a percentage of total population) have no significant effects on the net FDI inflows (as a percentage of GDP). The coefficient estimates along with the IRFs indicate that the results are robust across the two different measures of population ageing and the four panel VAR models.

6.5 Conclusion

Economic theory predicts a negative association between population ageing and net FDI inflows. Notwithstanding the importance of the negative association from theoretical and policy standpoints, few empirical studies have actually examined the direct effect of an increase in population ageing on foreign capital inflows. Using the most recent time series data from 1980 to 2017, this paper fills the gap in the existing literature by estimating a Bayesian panel VAR model for 22 OECD countries. To check for robustness, we have used two different measures of population ageing and have estimated four different models. The bivariate and the multivariate panel VAR analyses, along with the impulse response functions, indicate lack of any

Table 6.3 Multivariate bayesian panel VAR estimates

	(2)	(3)	(4)	(5)	(6)
Model 1	FDI	DRO	INV	OPN	RER
FDI (−1)	0.43(0.03)**	0.001 (0.00)	0.03 (0.01)**	0.08 (0.03)**	−0.03 (0.04)
FDI (−2)	0.10(0.03)**	0.0003 (0.00)	−0.03 (0.01)**	−0.06 (0.02)**	−0.03 (0.03)
DRO (−1)	−0.38(0.63)	1.93 (0.01)**	−0.08 (0.17)	−0.06 ((0.50)	−0.92 (0.71)
DRO (−2)	0.32(0.65)	−0.93 (0.01)**	0.07 (0.17)	0.05 (0.52)	0.93 (0.73)
INV (−1)	0.08(0.11)	−0.003 (0.00)	0.99 (0.03)**	−0.36 (0.09)**	0.21 (0.12)
INV (−2)	−0.13(0.10)	0.001 (0.00)	−0.14 (0.03)**	0.22 (0.08)**	−0.16 (0.12)
OPN (−1)	0.15(0.04)**	−0.0001 (0.00)	0.001(0.01)	0.95(0.03)**	−0.06(0.04)
OPN (−2)	−0.09 (0.04)**	0.0001(0.00)	−0.0002 (0.01)	0.06(0.03)**	0.07(0.04)
RER (−1)	0.01(0.03)	0.0001(0.00)	0.01(0.01)	−0.04(0.02)**	0.92(0.03)**
RER (−2)	−0.01(0.02)	−0.0002 (0.00)	−0.02(0.01)**	0.06(0.02)**	−0.07 (0.03)**
Constant	00.05(2.21)	0.07(0.03)**	4.72(0.58)**	1.73(1.76)	13.48(2.49)**
	(2)	(3)	(4)	(5)	(6)
Model 2	FDI	OLD	INV	OPN	RER
FDI (−1)	0.43(0.03)**	0.0004(0.00)	0.03(0.01)**	0.08(0.03)**	−0.03(0.04)
FDI (−2)	0.10(0.03)**	0.0001(0.00)	−0.03(0.01)**	−0.06(0.02)**	−0.03(0.03)
OLD (−1)	−1.10(1.17)	1.93(0.01)**	−0.16(0.31)	−0.45(0.94)	−2.03(1.33)
OLD (−2)	1.01(1.19)	−0.93(0.01)**	0.14(0.31)	0.43(0.95)	2.03(1.34)
INV (−1)	0.08(0.11)	−0.001(0.00)	0.99(0.03)**	−0.36(0.09)**	0.21(0.12)
INV (−2)	−0.13(0.10)	0.0004(0.00)	−0.13(0.03)**	0.22(0.08)**	−0.15(0.11)
OPN (−1)	0.15(0.04)**	−0.0001 (0.00)	0.001(0.01)	0.95(0.03)**	−0.06(0.04)
OPN (−2)	−0.09 (0.04)**	0.00004(0.00)	−0.0001 (0.01)	0.06(0.03)**	0.07(0.04)
RER (−1)	0.01(0.03)	0.00003(0.00)	0.01(0.01)	−0.04(0.02)**	0.92(0.03)**
RER (−2)	−0.01(0.02)	−0.0001 (0.00)	−0.02(0.01)**	0.06(0.02)**	−0.07 (0.03)**
Constant	0.19(2.22)	0.04(0.02)**	4.78(0.58)**	1.90(1.78)	13.62(2.52)**

The values in parenthesis represent standard errors
**Indicates significant at the 5% level

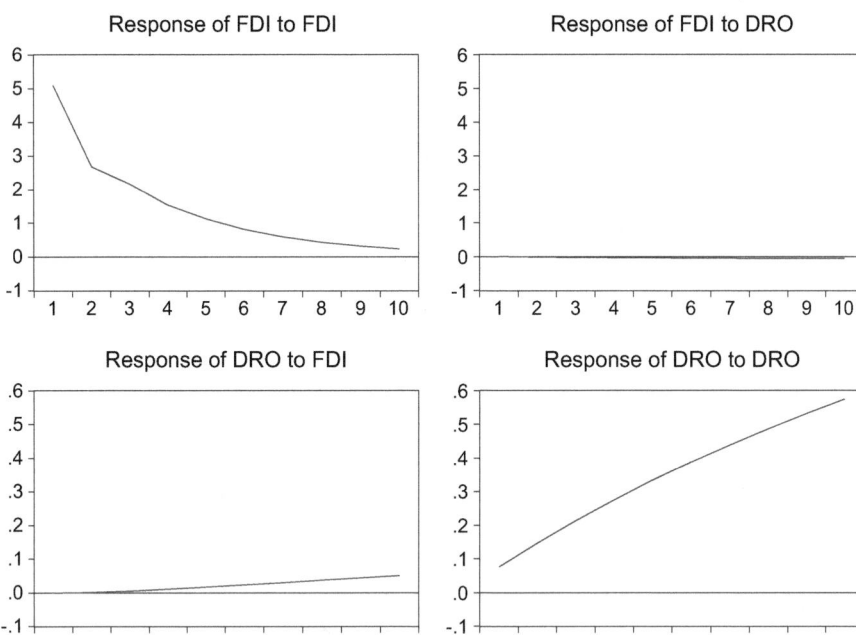

Fig. 6.2 Impulse response functions for bivariate model 1

significant relation between population ageing and net FDI inflows. We, therefore, conclude that an increase in population ageing will not significantly decrease net FDI inflows (as a percentage of GDP) into the sample of 22 OECD countries considered in our study.

References

Ando, A., & Modigliani, F. (1963). The life-cycle hypothesis of saving: Aggregate implications and tests. *American Economic Review, 53*(1), 55–84.

Choi, I. (2001). Unit root tests for panel data. *Journal of International Money and Finance, 20*(2), 249–272.

Donaldson, J. B., Koulovatianos, C., Li, J. & Mehra, R. (2018). *Demographics and FDI: Lessons from China's one-child policy, working paper 24256*, National Bureau of Economic Research.

Im, K. S., Pesaran, M. H., & Shin, Y. (2003). Testing for unit roots in heterogeneous panels. *Journal of Econometrics, 115*(1), 53–74.

Knickerbocker, F. T. (1973). *Oligopolistic reaction and multinational Enterprise* (Vol. 15, p. 7). Boston: Harvard University Press.

Levin, A., Lin, C. F., & Chu, C. J. (2002). Unit root tests in panel data: Asymptotic and finite sample properties. *Journal of Econometrics, 108*(1), 1–24.

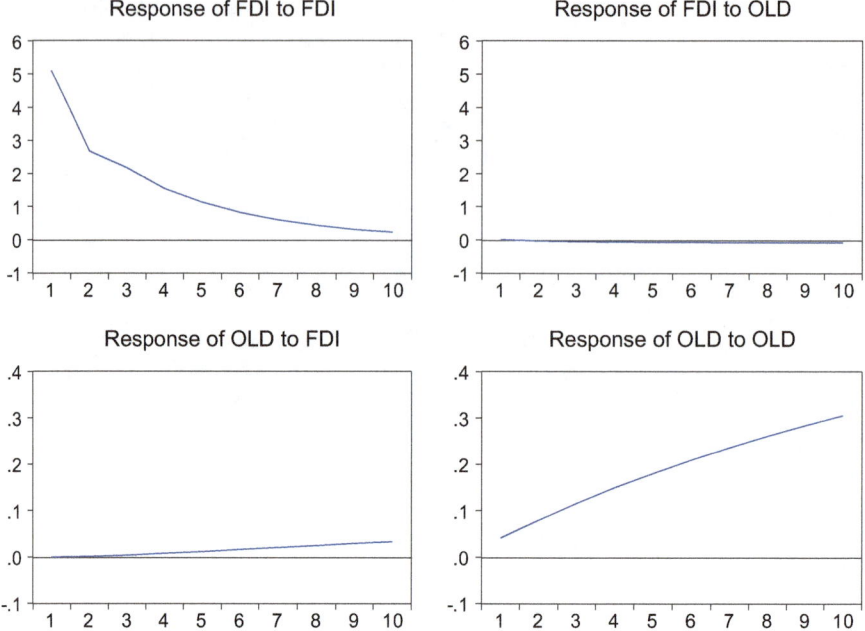

Fig. 6.3 Impulse response functions for bivariate model 2

Maddala, G. S., & Wu, S. (1999). A comparative study of unit root tests with panel data and a new simple test. *Oxford Bulletin of Economics and Statistics, 61*(S1), 631–652.

Mitra, R., & Abedin, T. (2020). *Population ageing and FDI inflows in OECD countries: A dynamic panel cointegration analysis. Discussion paper*. Japan: Tokyo International University.

Modigliani, F., & Brumberg, R. (1954). Utility analysis and the consumption function: An interpretation of cross-section data. In K. K. Kurihara (Ed.), *Post-Keynesian economics* (pp. 388–436). New Brunswick: Rutgers University Press.

Narciso, A. (2010). *The impact of population ageing on international capital flows. MPRA paper 26457*. Germany: University Library of Munich.

Vernon, R. (1966). International investment and international trade in the product cycle. *Quarterly Journal of Economics, 80*(2), 190–207.

Chapter 7
Productivity and Efficiency of Home-Based Enterprises in India: Evidence from NSS Data

Manik Kumar

7.1 Introduction

A significant proportion of output and employment are generated by informal sector in developing countries (Schneider et al. 2010). Approximately 48% of non-agricultural employment in North Africa, 51% in Latin America, 65% in Asia and 72% in sub-Saharan Africa are of informal in nature (ILO 2002). In context of India almost 90% of workers are informal worker. In addition, informal sector is a major contributor for national output in primary, secondary and tertiary sectors, and exports as well. For instance, contribution of informal sector is 40% of the total industrial output and 35% of total exports of India (CUTS 2003).

Given its significant contribution in the economy, it is essential to understand how productivity and efficiency of the informal sector's enterprises perform. From the economy's perspective, efficiency of informal sector's enterprises may be linked with productivity and efficiency of the whole economy because informal sector provides about 90% to total employment and contributes about 60% to Net Domestic Product (NDP). From the policy maker's perspective, knowledge of relative performance of enterprises in informal sector is important for current policy intervention.

However, quite a lot of researches have put their scholarly contributions on the subject and have tried to understand and measure the performance of organized manufacturing sector. In case of unorganized/informal sector, studies are not many that have focused on performance measurement. Rajesh and Duraisamy (2007) measured the technical efficiency and productivity performance of unorganized manufacturing enterprises across the states using Data Envelopment Analysis and National Sample Survey (NSS) data. Natarajan and Rajesh (2007) measured the technical efficiency levels in the unorganized manufacturing enterprises in Kerala

M. Kumar (✉)
Centre for Budget and Governance Accountability, New Delhi, Delhi, India

© The Author(s), under exclusive license to Springer Nature Switzerland AG 2021
A. K. Mishra et al. (eds.), *Advances in Innovation, Trade and Business*,
Contributions to Management Science,
https://doi.org/10.1007/978-3-030-60354-0_7

utilizing a stochastic production frontier approach using firm-level data for the period 2000–2001. Rajesh and Duraisamy (2007) analysed the size, growth and productivity performance of the unorganized manufacturing sector in India during 1978–1979 to 2000–2001. Total factor productivity growth in the unorganized manufacturing sector in India using several rounds of the large scale NSS state-level data for 15 major Indian states for the period 1978–1979 to 2000–2001 is measured by Rajesh and Duraisamy (2008). Kathuria et al. (2010) estimated state-wise performance of organized and unorganized manufacturing sector using various rounds of Annual Survey of Industry and NSS data, with deferent methodology. Sahu (2010) calculated the performance of unorganized manufacturing on the basis of subcontracted and non-subcontracted enterprises using crude measure of productivity.

Above studies on contribution in GDP, export, employment and growth of the unorganized sector need further analysis, because of two reasons. First, established research assumes all unorganized manufacturing enterprises are homogeneous on the basis of location, but it has high degree of heterogeneity on the basis of location and several other dimensions. Second, established studies are based on unorganized manufacturing only, but the unorganized service also contribute 75 to 91 per cent out of total service sector employment in India (Ghani et al. 2013).

For instance, a comparative analysis within the unorganized sectors on the basis of several dimensions may be relevant to fill these gaps. Therefore, the central objective of this paper is to analyse the performance of home-based enterprises to minimize the heterogeneity of unorganized sector.

In context of Indian data set (NSS Enterprises Rounds) on unorganized enterprises there are two type of enterprises, first is own account enterprises (operate without any hired labour on fairly regular basis) and second is establishments (operated with at least one hired labour). On the basis of type of enterprises there is a huge heterogeneity among them. Around 85% of total enterprises are own account enterprises they absorb more labour (at aggregate level) as compared to establishment, but on the other hand real gross value-added (GVA) and fixed asset (FA) per enterprises of own account enterprises are significantly low as compared to establishment over the period of time.[1] Gross value-added per worker are also significantly low for own account enterprises (OAE) as compared to their counter-part. That means most of OAE are working under distress situation as compared to establishment. But this explanation is so simple and it obscures many other aspects. There are high degrees of heterogeneity among OAE. Current study primarily divided all own account enterprises in two parts. First, Home-Based Enterprises (HBE): own account enterprises located within home and second, Non-Home-Based Enterprises (N-HBE): own account enterprises located outside home with fixed premises and with or without permanent/temporary structure. Home-based and non-home-based enterprises may be classified only on the basis of enterprises located either within or outside the premises of household as per definition proposed

---

[1]For detail data see Appendix 1.

by Delhi Group (GOI 2008). But notion of household contain fixed premises with any type of structure whether it is permanent and temporary. Definition proposed by Delhi Group (2007) primarily focuses on home-based worker; 'those who are doing remunerative work from home'. But any individual who are doing remunerative work within household premises for market basically operate an enterprise. So in the present study, we home-based enterprises located within household premises.

Around 42% of OAE are HBE and they absorb more labour as compared to N-HBE, but on the other hand real gross value-added (GVA) and fixed asset (FA) of HBE are significantly lower as compared to N-HBE over the period of time.[2] Gross values added per worker are also significantly low for HBE as compared to their counterpart. GVA of other enterprises[3] (enterprises involved in mobile marketing and street vendors) is higher than HBE but it has less fixed asset as well as worker per enterprises compared to HBE. That indicates working condition of HBE is significantaly worse than its counterpart. So present study focuses on HBE for detailed analysis, because it operates not only in distress situation but it contains significant number of enterprises, which has been growing faster and it absorb more labour also. Productivity performance of home-based enterprises has considerable importance because it is directly related to livelihood of household (home-based enterprises operate by all members of household) or home-based worker.

The plan of the rest of the paper is as follows. Section 7.2 discusses the methodology employed in the study. The database and variables used in the study are discussed in Sect. 7.3. Section 7.4 describes the partial and total factor productivity growth of home-based and non-home-based enterprises on different diminutions. The last section is conclusion.

7.2 Methodology

There are two frequently used measures of productivity. First is single factor productivity (SFP)/partial factor productivity (PFP) and second is total factor productivity (TFP). The partial factor productivity (or SFP) is defined as the ratio of value-added (or output) to the quantity of the factor input (e.g., labour productivity or capital productivity). When the proportion, in which all factors are used is same, then partial measure of productivity gives us vague results. In a condition where the capital–labour ratio pursues a rising tendency, the productivity of labour is overrated and productivity of capital as underestimated. For example, capital expanding can lead to an increase in labour and decrease in capital productivity over time. Likewise, advancement in labour productivity could also be due to adjustment in level of economies (Mahadevan 2004). In brief, the partial measure of productivity does not give in general changes in productive capacity because it is influenced by

---

[2]For detail data see Appendix 2.

[3]For basic comparison study also include other enterprises.

advancement in the composition of inputs. Despite the consequences, assessment of productivity of labour is quite necessary because it is directly related to welfare of society (Chen 1979). So in the present study, we estimate both partial and total factor productivity. Here, we are measuring technical, scale efficiency and total factor productivity growth in the following way:

$$\text{Total factor productivity growth (TFPG)} = \text{Technical efficiency} \times \text{Scale efficiency.}$$

There are two major techniques to compute TFP growth—frontier as well as non-frontier approaches. The fundamental dissimilarity among frontier and non-frontier path lies in the definition of frontier adopted by method. The aim of frontier method is to find bounding function. A 'cost frontier' indicates the minimum possible cost at given input prices and output, and a 'production frontier' expresses the set of maximum available output for a given set of inputs as well as technology. But in the case of non-frontier approach we assume the average function and then estimate ordinary least square regression. On the other hand frontier approach is based on technical efficiency of whole firm. But non-frontier approach is based on assumption of technically efficiency of firm. Parametric and non-parametric approach can be used for estimation of frontier as well as non-frontier. In case of parametric method, a categorical functional form is stated for the frontier and the parameters are predictable econometrically using data for inputs as well as output. But the accuracy of the resulting estimates is sensitive to the functional form specified. The main benefit of the parametric method is verification of econometrically estimated parameter on the basis of statistical test. But the major drawback of parametric approach is functional form that assumes neo-classical production function. Lovell (1993) argues that no technique is full proof for measurement of TFPG. Selection of a technique for measuring total factor productivity growth essentially depends on research question. Since the present study examines cause of TFPG, the frontier technique is more helpful because it breaks down TFPG into various apparatuses. A Data Envelope Analysis technique which is based on linear programming is used to construct the Malmquist productivity index for the HBE and N-HBE. The linear programming (LP) technique has two benefits over the econometric method in measuring TFPG (Grosskopf 1986). First, it analyze the condition to the 'best' performing rather than 'average' performed technology. Second, it 'does not require the specification of an *ad hoc* functional form or error structure'. In this procedure, the LP technique allows revival of various efficiency and productivity measures in a simply quantifiable manner. Malmquist Productivity index (MPI) was first investigated by Caves et al. (1982) and empirically used by Fare et al. in (1994).

The MPI is defined by using distance function. It measures TFPG among two data point by computing the ratio of detachment of each and every data point relative to a similar technology. Present study follow the Fare et al. (1994), output-oriented MPI:

$$M_0\left(x^{t+1},y^{t+1},x^t,y^t\right) = \left[\frac{D_0^t(x^{t+1},y^{t+1})}{D_0^t(x^t,y^t)} * \frac{D_0^{t+1}(x^{t+1},y^{t+1})}{D_0^{t+1}(x^t,y^t)}\right]^{\frac{1}{2}}.$$

A valve of M_0 greater than one indicates positive TFPG from period t to $t+1$ and vice versa. The Malmquist index has numerous features, which make it a powerful approach. First, it is a TFP index (Fare and Primont 1995). Second, it can be constructed via distance functions, which are primary measures, based only on input and output quantities rather than price. Third, the index can be decomposed into technical efficiency change, technical change and scale effect components. Efficiency change can be further decomposed into pure efficiency change and scale components. The technical change component can also be decomposed into pure technical change, input-based as well as output-based technical change components. As efficiency and technical changes are equivalent to the concept of technological innovation and adoption, respectively, the dynamics of the recent growth observed in the manufacturing sector of the Indian economy can be appreciated better. Finally, assumptions do not need to be made with regard to objectives of firms or regions in terms of, say, cost minimization or profit maximization objectives, which could be unsuitable in certain situations. But Malmquist index is not free from drawbacks. Its measurement error and statistical noises are assumed to be nonexistent, and it does not allow for statistical tests typical of the parametric approach. Malmquist productivity index basically sets a common technology for all observations and is best suited for firm-level analysis.

7.3   Data

Present study used different rounds of unit level NSS Enterprises data to estimate partial and total factor productivity growth. Data for the HBE in India is obtained from the nationally representative follow-up surveys of the National Sample Survey for the unorganized sector, namely, 55th round on Informal Non-Agricultural Enterprises 1999–2000, 67th round on unincorporated non-agricultural enterprises (excluding construction), 2010–2011 and 73th round on unincorporated non-agricultural enterprises (excluding construction) 2015–2016. In the present study we also include unorganized services enterprises. NSS includes services in above rounds only that are why we include these time periods in our analysis. It needs to be stated upfront that changes in sampling design and conceptual modifications introduced to accommodate requirement for improved data collection may, to an extent, affect the comparability of NSSO data over time (Kathuria et al. 2010). There are also differences across rounds in terms of coverage of the survey.

7.3.1   Variables

The variables used in this exercise are output, labour and capital inputs. To estimate the total factor productivity growth (TFPG) we could also include land and energy. But due to the lack of availability of adequate data we include gross value-added (GVA), fixed asset and number of worker in our analysis. To make the values of output and capital inputs comparable over time and across industries, suitable deflators have been used. The definition of the variables and the deflators used and various issues involved while selecting these variables are as given below.

7.3.1.1   Output

Two kinds of output measures can be used to calculate TFP and TFP growth: gross value-added and gross output. Present study uses GVA because at the industry level analysis GVA scores over gross output. The latter includes the cost of intermediate inputs which may vary greatly across industries (Diewert 2000). Use of value-added allows assessment among the firms that are using heterogeneous raw materials (Griliches and Ringsted 1971), and it too takes into account differences and changes in the quality of inputs. The present chapter uses gross value-added as a proxy of output because gross value-added at constant prices is a common practice in the Indian empirical literature (Unel 2003; Ahluwalia 1991; Balakrishnan and Pushpangadan 1998; and Goldar 1986) as well as lack of data availability for any other measure.[4]

Input

Present study uses capital (fixed asset) and labour as an input variable.

7.3.1.2   Capital

Measurement of capital input is the most composite among all input measurements in theoretical as well as empirical literature. There is no universally accepted method for its measurement and, as a result, several methods have been employed to estimate capital stock. There are mainly two methods of measurement of capital input one is the book value of the fixed asset and another is the perpetual inventory method (PIM). The book value method has three limitations. First, the use of 'lumpy' capital data which might be underestimates or overestimates the amount of capital expenditure. Second, the book value may never accurately characterize the physical stock of machinery and equipment used in the production. Third, it does not deal with the question of capacity utilization. The Perpetual inventory method also does not address the question of capacity utilization. Despite this limitation the present study follows Ray (2002) and uses book value of the total fixed asset as reported

---

[4]NSSO gases only gross value-added data.

in NSSO to represent capital input in the HBE. The total fixed assets were deflated by WPI for machine and machinery tools at base 2011–2012. The WPI for the machine and machinery tools are not available at the industry level, but for the sake of simplicity the present study assumes that machine uses in different industry are homogeneous.

7.3.1.3 Labour

The usual technique of measuring labour input is either to use the number of hours worked or the number of workers employed. The appropriate labour measure would require incorporating the quality of the labour inputs accounting for the sex, education, employment status of the worker, etc. (Mahadevan, 2003). A total number of persons engaged in the production process are treated as labour input, irrespective of proprietors, owners and supervisors. Managerial staffs have a significant influence on the productivity of a firm, but for the sake of simplicity and lack of appropriate data availability (especially in NSS) the present study uses number of persons engaged as a labour input in unorganized sector. The present chapter makes a small modification in the worker in unorganized sector following GOI (2008),[5] i.e. considers two part-time workers as one full-time worker.

7.3.2 Appropriate Deflator

If value-added is used as a measure of output, nominal value needs to be transformed into real value-added. This conversion can be done with either single deflation (SD) or double deflation (DD) method. In the case of the SD, nominal gross value-added is deflated by the output price index, i.e., both nominal output and nominal material inputs are deflated by the output price index. But the SD method assumes that both material price and output price change at the same rate. To avoid this difficulty, it has been recommended that it is better to deflate output and material input separately (for each industry) and then works out the real value-added (Balakrishnan and Pushpangadan 1994). The single deflator method is sensitive to change in the index. During the periods when the input price index increases at a faster rate than the output price index, the estimate of real value-added obtained by using the SD method will be lower than that obtained by using DD method and vice versa. However, this method has been criticized on the ground that reliable estimates of input price indices for the unorganized sector are not available due to the problem of finding appropriate weights. Since our study is covering the period following the 2000s reforms, when the economy was being further integrated into the world economy, the industries must be experiencing large relative price changes,

---

[5]For detailed explanation please see NCEUS report.

significant changes in factor shares and large changes in the value of inputs relative to output. In this context of transition, the use of the DD procedure would be more ideal than the SD procedure. In this study, we deflate gross value-added and fixed asset by overall WPI and index of machine and machinery tools, respectively. To deflate GVA and fixed asset WPI overall and WPI machine and machinery tools, respectively, are more appropriate in place of CPI (Balakrishnan and Pushpangadan 1994).

7.4 Partial and Total Factor Productivity Growth Productivity of Home-Based Enterprises

In the present study, we estimate both partial and total factor productivity growth for home-based, non-home-based and other type of enterprises (Street vendors and Mobile marketing). To check the robutness of the study we comapred street vending enterprises with HBE and N-HBE. But this study primarily focuses on home-based enterprises. At initial level, it is better to compare home-based enterprises with non-home-based and enterprises involved in street vending/mobile marketing. So, to understand the basic characteristics of these kinds of enterprises the present study estimates partial productivity of all three types of enterprises over the period of time.

Several key structural ratios must be considered to explain the performance differences between the home-based and non-home-based small enterprises. Structural coefficients such as labour productivity, capital intensity and worker per enterprises provide considerable insights about the relative efficiency of enterprises that are working as home-based and others that are not. The value addition capacity of home-based enterprises depends on the type of technology in use, nature of activity done by these enterprises, type of ownership and nature of subcontracting.

At the aggregate level, per worker productivity of home-based enterprises was estimated at Rs 26,026, Rs 35,884 and Rs 50,137 for 1999–2000, 2010–2011 and 2015–2016. respectively (Table 7.1). But per worker productivity of non-home-based enterprises was significantly higher over the period of time, i.e. Rs 51,153, Rs 68,945 and Rs 97,751 for 1999–2000, 2010–2011 and 2015–2016, respectively. Average labour productivity in home-based enterprises is not only lower as compared with non-home-based enterprises, but its growth is also considerably low. Table 7.1 also shows labour productivity of home-based enterprises appreciably low as compared to enterprises involved in street vending and mobile marketing over the period of time. On the other hand growth of labour productivity is very low in case of home-based enterprises among all three types of enterprises. The relatively low labour productivity of the home-based enterprises as compared with the non-home-based enterprises may be attributed to the use of labour intensive and outdated technology. Home-based enterprises also have inadequate access to both output and input market, proliferation of middlemen and adverse market conditions.

Table 7.1 Partial productivity by enterprises category

	Labour productivity	Capital intensity	Worker per enterprises
	1999–2000		
HBE	26,026	26,845	1.59
N-HBE	51,153	79,549	1.50
Other	43,398	15,436	1.15
	2010–2011		
HBE	35,884	89,841	1.54
N-HBE	68,945	225,477	1.44
Other	53,505	56,743	1.10
	2015–2016		
HBE	50,137	51,936	1.45
N-HBE	97,751	101,259	1.32
Other	82,255	85,206	1.14

Note: HBE Home-based enterprises, *N-HBE* Non-home-based enterprises, *Other* Mobile marketing and Street vendors. Per worker productivity and capital–labour ratio are in rupees at constant 2011–2012 prices
Source: Author estimation form various enterprises round of NSSO unit level data

At the aggregate level, capital intensity of home-based enterprises was estimated at Rs 26,845, Rs 89,841 and Rs 51,936 for 1999–2000, 2010–2011 and 2015–2016, respectively (Table 7.1). But capital intensity of non-home-based enterprises was significantly high over the period of time, i.e. Rs 79,549, Rs 225,477 and Rs 101,259 for 1999–2000, 2010–2011 and 2015–2016, respectively. Average capital intensity in home-based enterprises is not only lower as compared with non-home-based enterprises, but it also has negative growth during 2010–2011 to 2015–2016. Table 7.1 also explains capital intensity was less for enterprises involved in street vending and mobile marketing among all types of enterprise over the period of time (except 2015–2016), but per labour productivity was considerably higher as compared to home-based enterprises. Thus, home-based enterprises operate with more capital and labour as compared to all three kinds of enterprises. But it has less productivity in terms of labour, as compared to not only non-home-based worker but also enterprises involved in street vending or mobile marketing.

However, the home-based enterprises have potential to generate employment with lower capital. On an average, the employment content of home-based enterprises is considerably higher than that of non-home-based as well as enterprises involved in street vending, over the period of time. While every home-based enterprises on an average employed 1.45 persons against 1.32 by a non home-based enterprises (Fig. 7.1).

It is important to know whether the growth in the home-based enterprises has involved efficient use of resources. The partial factor productivities such as labour and capital are not sufficient indicators of efficiency, because increase in labour productivity could be due to change in the capital–labour ratios. Partial measure of productivity such as labour productivity and capital intensity does not provide a clear picture of overall productivity performance of enterprises as it hides many things.

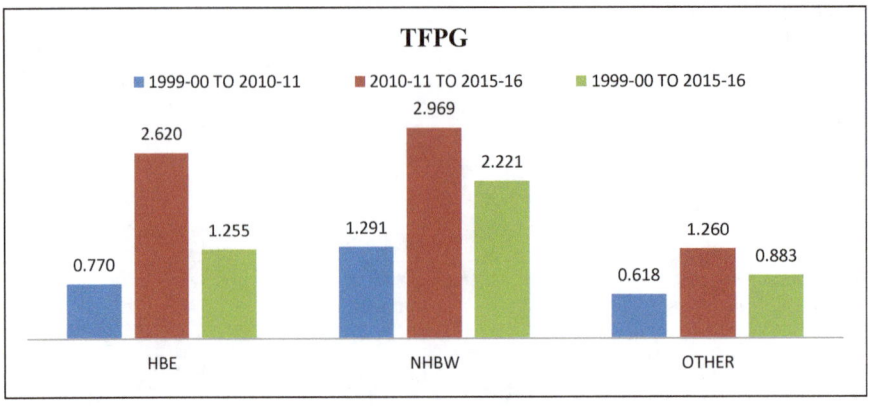

Fig. 7.1 Total factor productivity growth of home-based enterprises and its counterpart. *Source:* As cited in Table 7.1

The total factor productivity growth (TFPG), or technical change, captures growth in value-added not accounted for by the growth in inputs such as labour and capital. TFP growth is a residual productivity growth and includes the effect of technological changes, better utilization of capacities, skills and organization. So, to analyze the overall productive performance of enterprises, we estimate total factor productivity growth, scale and technical efficiency of home-based, non home-based and enterprises involve in street vending and mobile marketing. The non-home-based enterprises had relatively high total factor productivity growth at 2.22 point the study period as compared to home-based enterprises. Total factor productivity growth of all kinds of enterprises had growth during 2010–2011, but TFPG of home-based enterprises still below as compared to its counterpart (Fig. 7.2).

The non-home-based enterprises had relatively high scale efficiency at 1.65% the study period as compared to home-based enterprises. Scale efficiency of all types of enterprises had grown during 2010–11, but scale efficiency of home-based enterprises still below as compare to its non home-based enterprises.

Technical efficiency is the effectiveness with which a given set of inputs is used to produce an output. A firm is said to be technically efficient if they are producing the maximum output from the minimum quantity of inputs, such as labour, capital and technology. Technical efficiency follow the same pattern like scale efficiency and total factor productivity growth. Technical efficiency of home-based enterprises was estimated 0.741, 1.658 and 0.928 during 1999–2000 to 2010–2011, 2010–2011 to 2015–2016 and 1999–2000 to 2015–2016, respectively (Fig. 7.3).

Thus, above explanation proves that home-based enterprises working in more suffering situation as compared to non-home-based as well as enterprises involved in street vending and mobile marketing. The prime goal of the present study is to understand the dynamics and characteristics of home-based enterprises. So, this aggregate picture needs to be disaggregated because it is very heterogeneous. It

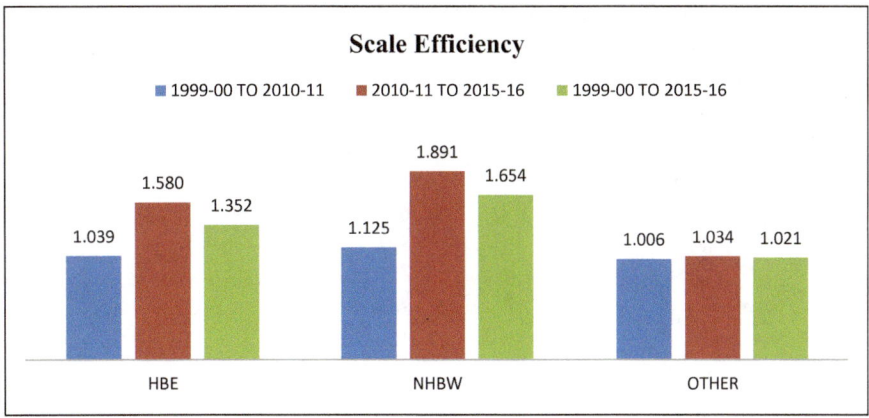

Source: As cited in Table1.

Fig. 7.2 Scale efficiency of home-based enterprises and its counterpart. *Source:* As cited in Table 7.1

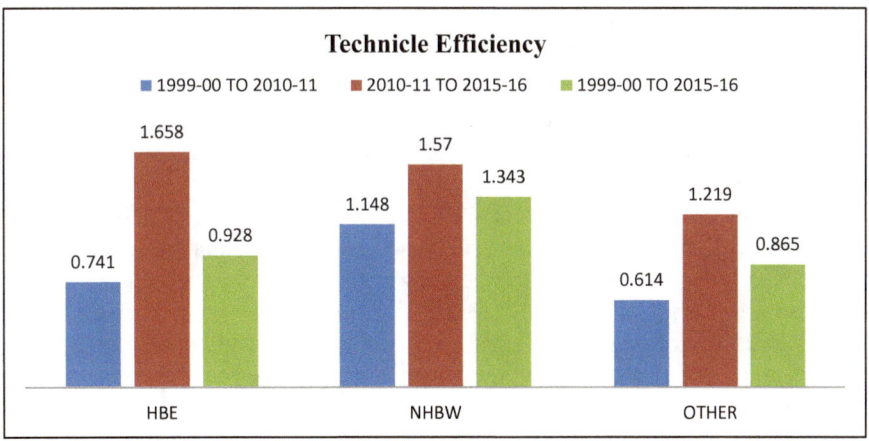

Source: As cited in Table1.

Fig. 7.3 Technical efficiency of home-based enterprises and its counterpart. *Source:* As cited in Table 7.1

might be possible that the productivity of different segments of OAE may different. So, in the present study we estimate partial and total factor productivity at HBE at disaggregated level.

There has been enormous disparity between operational and other dynamics of enterprises that operate different sectors like rural and urban. These geographical locations significantly influence the labour productivity and capital intensity over the period of time. Labour productivity of home-based enterprises in rural areas was estimated in Rs 21,382, Rs 29,581 and Rs 41,443 for 1999–2000, 2010–2011 and

Table 7.2 Partial productivity of HBE by sector

	Labour productivity	Capital intensity	Worker per enterprises
	1999–2000		
Rural	21,382	17,290	1.60
Urban	37,945	51,368	1.56
	2010–2011		
Rural	29,581	48,665	1.61
Urban	47,515	165,817	1.41
	2015–2016		
Rural	41,443	42,930	1.37
Urban	64,787	67,112	1.33

Source: As cited in Table 7.1

2015–2016, respectively (Table 7.2). Labour productivity of home-based enterprises has considerably higher in urban area as compared to enterprises located in rural areas. Labour productivity of home-based enterprises located in urban area not only high but it is growing faster than rural home-based enterprises. The same pattern was followed in case of capital intensity, an urban home-based enterprise has high capital intensity over the period of time and it is also growing faster than rural home-based enterprises. But labour absorption capacity in terms of per enterprises is high for rural as compared to urban home-based enterprises. Table 7.2 shows there have relatively more labour engaged in rural as compared to urban home-based enterprises over the period of time.

At the all-India level, the total factor productivity growth was high during 2010–2011 to 2015–2016 periods in rural and urban areas, but average total factor productivity growth during the study period was estimated 1.589 and 2.424 point for rural and urban areas, respectively (Table 7.3). Total factor productivity growth of home-based enterprise operate in urban areas was higher than its counterpart over the study period. Total factor productivity growth in urban home-based enterprises is not only higher as compared to rural home-based enterprises, but it has also grown faster during the study period (15 years). Scale and technical efficiency of urban home-based worker is also considerably high as compared with rural home-based enterprises.

This proves that rural home-based enterprises are more labour intensive than urban. Because of labour intensive technique used by rural home-based enterprises has low labour productivity growth as compare to urban enterprises. Rural home-based enterprises operate with more labour and less capital; they have less access to market, technology and credit, etc. that is why they have less total factor productivity growth and efficency as compared to urban home-based enterprise (Table 7.4).

Indian society has strong segmentation on the basis of gender. Female has to follow strong social and cultural norms as compared to male member in the same society. Thus, female in Indian society do not have adequate access to market; credit, technology and other things which support any individual to establish or run an enterprise in proper manner. So, gender has significant impact of entrepreneurial

Table 7.3 Total factor productivity and efficiency (scale and technical) of home-based enterprises by sector

	1999–2000 to 2010–2011	2010–2011 to 2015–2016	1999–2000 to 2015–2016
	Scale efficiency		
Rural	1.028	1.259	1.621
Urban	1.096	1.136	1.891
	Technical efficiency		
Rural	0.605	1.587	0.98
Urban	0.946	1.738	1.282
	Total factor productivity growth		
Rural	0.622	1.998	1.589
Urban	1.037	1.974	2.424

Source: As cited in Table 7.1

Table 7.4 Partial productivity of HBE by ownership type

	Labour productivity	Capital intensity	Worker per enterprises
	1999–2000		
Male owned	30,264	30,607	1.66
Female owned	13,330	15,797	1.35
	2010–2011		
Male owned	45,995	106,480	1.48
Female owned	21,466	69,800	1.24
	2015–2016		
Male owned	64,885	67,213	1.45
Female owned	29,371	30,425	1.18

Source: As cited in Table 7.1

capacity in Indian society. These entrepreneurial capacities have direct and positive impact on productivity performance of enterprises run by them. Labour productivity of home-based enterprises run by male was estimated in Rs 30,264, Rs 45,995 and Rs 64,885 for 1999–2000, 2010–2011 and 2015–2016, respectively (Table 7.3). On the other hand labour productivity of female owned enterprises was estimated Rs 13,330, Rs 21,466 and Rs 29,371 for the same period of time, which is considerably lower as compared to their counterpart during the overall study periods.

Total factor productivity growth of male owned home-based enterprises was estimated 0.835, 2.76% for 1999–2011 and 2011–2016, respectively (Table 7.5). Total factor productivity of female owned enterprises is not only less as compared to male owned home-based enterprises but its growth is also almost constant during the study period. Female owned home-based enterprises is less technical and scale efficient as compared with male owned home-based enterprises.

Relatively less partial and total factor productivity growth of female owned home-based enterprises as compared with their counterpart over the period of time has been low, that proves female has low entrepreneurial capacity. This less entrepreneurial capacity may be because of limited access to market and other

Table 7.5 Total factor productivity and efficiency (scale and technical) of home-based enterprises by type of ownership

	1999–2000 to 2010–2011	2010–2011 to 2015–2016	1999–2000 to 2015–2016
	Scale efficiency		
Male owned	1.035	1.268	1.324
Female owned	0.816	1.186	1.064
	Technical efficiency		
Male owned	0.807	1.76	1.192
Female owned	0.679	1.92	1.192
	Total factor productivity growth		
Male owned	0.835	2.760	1.578
Female owned	0.554	2.277	1.268

Source: As cited in Table 7.1

facilities for female, which might enhance productivity performance of HBE in Indian society.

Such kinds of explanations are also true in case of social groups in Indian society. In general, caste and income strata are almost overlapping in Indian society (it is not exactly overlapped in now days). There has been a bunch of research that is arguing discrimination in access to resources and its utilization on the basis of caste in Indian economy as well as society. In general, established literatures on caste-based discrimination suggest forward caste has more opportunity than other backward and SC/STs. Thus, in the present study we hypothesize home-based enterprises owned by forward caste has more efficient than other caste, i.e. other backward and SC/STs.

The present study estimates partial and total factor productivity of home-based enterprises owned by different social groups. There has been limitation of data, information regarding social group of owner is provided only in 67th (2010–2011) and 73rd (2015–2016). So in this study we estimate all coefficients only for previous 5 years. Table 7.6 shows labour productivity of home-based enterprises owned by forward caste was estimated Rs 59,922 for 2015–2016, that is more among other. Upper caste owned home-based enterprises use capital intensive technique (Tables 7.6 and 7.7).

Total factor productivity growth and technical efficiency of upper caste owned home-based enterprises was estimated 1.905 point during the study periods, which is considerably high as compared to home-based enterprises owned by OBCs and SC/STs.

High partial and total productivity with efficiency of home-based enterprises owned by upper caste compared with lower caste over the period of time prove upper caste has more access and/or owned capital asset, market and technology to operate an enterprises in proper way. Such kinds of access to facilities generate

Table 7.6 Partial productivity of HBE by social group of owner

	Labour productivity	Capital intensity	Worker per enterprises
	2010–2011		
SC/ST	29,423	53,648	1.46
OBC	36,540	86,941	1.44
GEN	42,939	126,495	1.33
	2015–2016		
SC/ST	37,182	38,516	1.41
OBC	49,548	51,326	1.37
GEN	59,922	62,072	1.28

Source: As cited in Table 7.1

Table 7.7 Total factor productivity and efficiency (scale and technical) of home-based enterprises by social group

	2010–2011 to 2015–2016		
	Scale Efficiency	Technical Efficiency	TFPG
SC/ST	1.038	1.298	1.347
OBC	1.289	1.409	1.816
GEN	1.145	1.664	1.905

Source: As cited in Table 7.1

entrepreneurial capacity in individual who belong to upper caste. But this entrepreneurial capacity does not create in lower caste because of caste-based discrimination and social cultural norms.

7.5 Subcontracting

There is a huge debate in literature on productivity and efficiency of subcontracted and non-subcontracted manufacturing enterprises. The early empirical literature on India argued that the subcontracting inter-firm linkages were exploitative: the workers were paid low wages, did not receive any benefits, and the nature of work did not allow them to organize themselves, thus reducing their bargaining power (Bose 1978; Harriss 1982; Banerjee 1988). However, the more recent literature on subcontracting in India argues that this is an efficient form of production organization, though there is an implicit mention of the attendant exploitation of labour (Basant and Chandra 2002; Morris and Basant 2004). But these researches are not conclusive in terms of subcontracting, because, these all are fuscous only on manufacturing. The exploitative nature of work within the subcontracting chain is more likely to occur in informal enterprises essentially home-based situations. Thus, this section of present study we fuscous on effect of subcontracting on productivity of home based enterprises.

Home- based enterprises working under subcontracting with both kinds of firms whether it is traditional and modern. So, before analyzing the productivity performance of subcontracted and non-subcontracted home-based enterprises the present study explains the theoretical system of subcontracting.

One of the key aspects in understanding the development of the informal sector is its interaction with the formal sector (Davies and Thurlow 2010; Hart 1973; Ranis and Stewart 1999). Two contrasting views that appear in the literature on informality are analysed empirically by capturing the diversity of informal sector activities through admeasures of informal sector modernity. The first view, hereafter referred to as the *stagnation view*, contends that formal enterprises subcontract the most labour-intensive production activities to traditional informal enterprises, in order to minimize labour costs. Due to intense pressure for cost competition exerted on informal enterprises, the linkages between formal and informal enterprises result in a downward spiral of wages, worsening labour conditions and the recreation of the survivalist characteristics of informal enterprises (Portes 2014; Tokman 1978). If this is the case, subcontracting linkages will be strongest between the formal sector and the most traditional segment of the informal sector, such that an increase in formal sector subcontracting nourishes traditional informal activities, thus contributing to stagnation of the informal sector.

The second view, labeled as the *modernization view*, holds that subcontracting is a vehicle for the modernization of the informal sector. Formal enterprises, therefore, only establish subcontracting relationships with modern informal enterprises, which can not only reduce the costs of production, but also ensure certain standards regarding quality of output and delivery times. Growth of the modern segment of the informal sector, or modernization of the informal sector, is positively related to the growth of the formal sector due to production linkages between the two (Marjit, 2003; Ranis and Stewart, 1999).

According to the *stagnation view*, formal enterprises wishing to reduce labour costs subcontract activities to informal enterprises. By their superior status in terms of size and capital, formal enterprises are able to impose stringent conditions on informal enterprises regarding prices, thus extracting most of the value-added and leaving informal enterprises stagnated in a survivalist mode (Portes 2014; Moser 1978; Portes and Shleifer 2014; Sanyal 2007; Tokman 1978). In fact, formal enterprises can benefit from the 'race-to-the bottom' in terms of labour costs in the informal sector, as it directly translates into higher profitability from subcontracting. As stagnant, survivalist informal enterprises are part of the traditional segment of the informal sector; an increase in the incidence of subcontracting would result in expansion of the traditional segment and thus work against the modernization of the informal sector.

A second view on the effects of subcontracting referred to as the *modernization view* holds that formal enterprises engage in subcontracting relationships only with modern informal enterprises. An explanation for this can be offered based on three complementary aims that formal enterprises pursue when engaging in subcontracting. The first one is to minimize costs so that the price of the subcontracted activity is as low as possible. The second one is to maximize the

Table 7.8 Partial productivity of HBE by subcontracting

	Labour productivity	Capital intensity	Worker per enterprises
	1999–2000		
Subcontracted	16,498	14,201	1.61
Non-subcontracted	28,631	30,303	1.58
	2010–11		
Subcontracted	17,925	34,322	1.45
Non-subcontracted	38,604	98,253	1.55
	2015–2016		
Subcontracted	25,557	26,475	1.29
Non-subcontracted	56,391	58,415	1.37

Source: As cited in Table 7.1

quality of the subcontracted product so as not to compromise the quality standards of the final product. The third one is to minimize the risk of vertically disintegrating the production process, so that the decision of subcontracting does not compromise the delivery time of the final product. Therefore, formal enterprises take into account not only the difference in costs between in-house production and subcontracting but also the productive and technological capacity of potential suppliers (Wattanapruttipaisan, 2002).

Partial productivity of non-subcontracted home-based enterprises is higher as compared to subcontract enterprises over the period of time (Table 7.8). But per enterprises labour involvement is high in non-subcontracted as compared with subcontract. Total factor productivity is also high in case of non-subcontracted home-based enterprises (Table 7.9).

Home-based enterprises are also not homogeneous on the basis of subcontracting. There are two types of home-based enterprises on the basis of subcontracting. First, those who are working on fully subcontracting system, means they produced all output for subcontractor and second is partially subcontracted, those who produce some of total output for subcontractor and the rest of it for market. So in the present study, we segmented subcontracted home-based enterprises in fully and partially subcontracted enterprises, and then estimated partial and total productivity for both segments.

At the aggregate level labour productivity in fully subcontracted home-based enterprises was estimated at Rs 14,538, Rs 17,486 and Rs 24,141 for 1999–2000, 2010–2011 and 2015–2016, respectively (Table 7.10). On the other hand, labour productivity in partially subcontracted home-based enterprises was estimated at Rs 31,072, Rs 22,511 and Rs 37,982 for 1999–2000, 2010–2011 and 2015–2016, respectively.

Capital–labour ratios, however, are lower in fully subcontracting home-based unit compared with partially subcontracting units over the period of time. Thus, the partially subcontracting home-based enterprises have more potential to generate employment with lower capital. On an average, the employment content of partially

Table 7.9 Total factor productivity and efficiency (scale and technical) of home-based enterprises who are working on subcontracting

	1999–2000 TO 2010–2011	2010–2011 TO 2015–2016	1999–2000 TO 2015–2016
	Scale efficiency		
Subcontracted	1.058	1.081	1.025
Non-subcontracted	1.068	1.028	1.342
	Technical efficiency		
Subcontracted	0.533	1.793	0.978
Non-subcontracted	0.815	1.88	1.238
	Total factor productivity growth		
Subcontracted	0.564	1.823	1.002
Non-subcontracted	0.870	1.933	1.661

Source: As cited in Table 7.1

Table 7.10 Partial productivity of HBE by type of subcontracting

	Labour productivity	Capital intensity	Worker per enterprises
	1999–2000		
Fully subcontracted	14,538	11,461	1.61
Partial subcontracted	31,072	32,705	1.64
	2010–2011		
Fully subcontracted	17,486	32,189	1.43
Partial subcontracted	22,511	56,561	1.60
	2015–2016		
Fully subcontracted	24,141	25,008	1.28
Partial subcontracted	37,982	39,345	1.38

Source: As cited in Table 7.1

subcontracting home-based enterprise marginally higher than that of fully subcontracting home-based unit.

Total factor productivity growth and efficiency of Partial Subcontracted home-based enterprises is significantly high over the period of time (Table 7.11). These differences in productivity performance between fully and partially subcontracted home based enterprises because of degree of dependency on parent unit. In general there are three types of input providing relation established in empirical literature; first: all factor of production like row material, equipment, etc. except labour provided by subcontractor, second: home-based worker/enterprises have to purchase all kinds of input from open market and third is mix of first and second. Fully Subcontracted home-based worker/enterprises have fully dependent on parent unit for row material, equipment, credit and other factor of production except labour, these dependencies on parent firms propel subcontracted home-based enterprises less productive and efficient. Fully dependency of home-based enterprises on parent

Table 7.11 Total factor productivity and efficiency (scale and technical) of home-based enterprises by nature of subcontracting

	1999–2000 to 2010–2011	2010–2011 to 2015–2016	1999–2000 to 2015–2016
	Scale efficiency		
Fully subcontracted	1.023	1.002	1.021
Partial subcontracted	1.058	1.095	1.032
	Technical efficiency		
Fully subcontracted	0.501	1.747	0.935
Partial subcontracted	0.686	1.891	1.139
	Total factor Productivity growth		
Fully subcontracted	0.511	1.750	0.954
Partial subcontracted	0.726	2.070	1.175

Source: As cited in Table 7.1

firm generate various dimensions and high degree of exploitation in terms of rumination, but the present study concerns about within enterprises dynamics, so exploitation is not discussed here.

In recent era home-based worker/enterprises are working in manufacturing, trading and services industry. Home-based enterprises are working in traditional manufacturing like manufacturing of food and beverages, tobacco product, garment, etc. On the other hand they also work in semi-modern wholesale and retail trade and modern services such as hotels and restaurants, transport, storage and communication, financial intermediation, health, education, etc. After the economic reform, there has been a significant concentration of home-based workers/ enterprises in services sector in India.

All these three industries are highly heterogeneous within and between industrial groups. So, in present study we estimated partial and total productivity separately for each industrial groups to check the between industrial groups heterogeneity. These three industries are not strangely comparable with each other. There has been productivity deference among them naturally. But in the present study we keep own account enterprises located within home (HBE), they are operate with more or less same feature, so in the present study we assume all home-based enterprises are similar or less heterogeneous across the industry. But estimation of total factor productivity might be fall in 'Industrial biased' due to this assumption. However, within industrial group heterogeneity still exist in analysis.

Table 7.12 shows manufacturing home-based enterprises has lower labour productivity and also lower capital intensity as compared with their counterpart over the period of time. But number of labour engaged per enterprises in manufacturing is relatively more or negligible fewer as compared with other trading and services

Table 7.12 Partial productivity of HBE by industry groups

	2010–2011			2015–2016		
	Labour productivity	Capital intensity	Worker/ENT	Labour productivity	Capital intensity	Worker/ENT
Manufacturing	25,526	60,860	1.44	35,130	36,390	1.33
Electricity, gas and water supply	35,540	51,821	1.51	43,658	45,224	1.22
Wholesale and retail trade	46,355	101,579	1.49	61,630	63,841	1.52
Transport, storage and communication	70,643	139,963	1.06	97,785	101,294	1.07
Hotels and restaurants	38,895	90,407	1.66	62,148	64,378	1.75
Information and technology	22,942	104,120	1.21	96,156	99,606	1.27
Financial intermediation	22,725	34,181	3.87	147,218	152,500	1.40
Real estate	70,598	812,250	1.03	94,524	97,916	1.03
Other business activities	77,321	214,800	1.30	103,995	107,727	1.25
Education	41,725	134,362	1.05	56,029	58,040	1.04
Health and social work	72,056	157,857	1.11	103,246	106,951	1.08
Other	37,693	91,038	1.33	55,976	57,985	1.29

Source: As cited in Table 7.1

home-based enterprises over the period of time, this is primarily because of manufacturing is more labour intensive as compared to other. Labour absorption capacity of manufacturing home-based enterprises is moderately high as compared to most of services sector home-based enterprises. But many services industries like wholesale, retail trade and hotels & restaurants has on an average more labour absorption capacity as compared to manufacturing enterprises over the period of time.

Total factor productivity growth, technical and scale efficiency of home-based enterprises for each industrial segmentation are reported in Table 7.13. Total factor productivity of manufacturing home-based enterprise was estimated 2.139 point during the study periods, which is high as compared with other home-based enterprises in services industry except hotels and restaurants, information and technology and education.

Scale efficiency for home-based manufacturing enterprise was estimated 1.35 point over the period of time, which is high as compared with other home-based enterprises in services industry except information and technology and education. But technical efficiency of services including trading home-based enterprises is significantly high as compared to manufacturing home-based enterprises over the study periods. Low labour productivity, less capital intensive but relatively high total

Table 7.13 Total factor productivity and efficiency (scale and technical) of home-based enterprises by industrial group

2010–2011 to 2015–2016			
	Scale Efficiency	Technical Efficiency	TFPG
Manufacturing	1.352	1.582	2.139
Electricity, gas and water supply	1.012	1.571	1.57
Wholesale and retail trade	1.152	1.725	1.986
Transport, storage and communication	1.154	1.803	1.803
Hotels and restaurants	1.243	1.705	2.119
Information and technology	2.122	1.839	3.904
Financial intermediation	1.020	1.740	1.774
Real estate	1.128	1.793	1.793
Other business activities	1.003	1.809	1.815
Education	1.570	1.709	2.684
Health and social work	1.008	1.811	1.825
Other	1.288	1.665	2.145

Source: As cited in Table 7.1

factor productivity growth of manufacturing home-based enterprises because of high scale efficiency.

7.6   Conclusion

Estimated number of enterprises operating without any hired worker at fairly regular basis has been grown significantly over the period of time. This paper has examined the productivity and efficiency (scale and technical) performance of home-based enterprises in India at different segmented levels such as sector (rural and urban), gender and social group of ownership, working on subcontracting and two digit NIC classification. Home-based enterprises operate with low capital base as compared to counterparts. But, it absorbed relatively more labour per enterprise. It shows that home-based enterprises have potential to generate more employment with relatively less capital. These enterprises do not hire worker, and therefore are basically family or household enterprises. Consequently, their productivity level is directly associated with livelihood of respective household. If home-based enterprises perform well in terms of productivity and operate efficiently, it may create better and sustainable livelihood avenues for the household. However, total factor productivity growth of home-based enterprises is half of their counterparts over the period of time, though it has increased significantly during 2010–2011 to 2015–2016 as compared to previous period. Sharp rise in productivity of home-based enterprises during above period may be because of macro-economy performed well during this time. Scale efficiency of home-based enterprises was also low as compared to non-home-based enterprises, proving that home-based enterprises do not efficiently organize their productive resources in production process. Technical efficiency of home-based enterprise was also low during this period, which means they were not using their resources optimally. These enterprises are characterized by high degree of heterogeneity and therefore any gross judgment runs the risks of over simplification. Therefore, total factor productivity growth at disaggregated level is estimated among home-based enterprises on the basis of ownership type, sector and subcontracting. It is shown that home-based enterprises owned by SC/ST, female and located in rural area had significantly low productivity compared with their counterpart. A significant number of home-based enterprises are working on contract basis, especially in manufacturing industry. Subcontracting itself has its own dynamics and affects productivity performance of enterprises through efficiency. In case of home-based enterprises subcontracting does not plays positive role to enhance their productivity. But it has negative impact on such kinds of enterprises, partly because home-based enterprises are too small to have any bargaining power. Degree of subcontracting (partially and fully) is also negatively related to productivity performance of home-based enterprises. Therefore, subcontracting does not help at all in augmenting livelihood of households. Moreover, now home-based enterprises have expanded to sectors other than manufacturing. Yet, manufacturing home-based enterprises have higher productivity as compared to services and trading, except HBE involved in information and technology and education.

Appendix 1

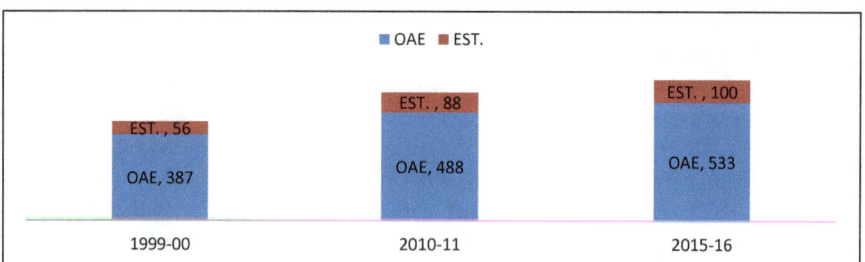

Source: Author Estimation form various Enterprises round of NSSO unit level Data.

Fig. 7.4 Estimated number of enterprises by enterprises type *(in lakhs)* by sector. *Source:* author estimation form various enterprises round of NSSO unit level data

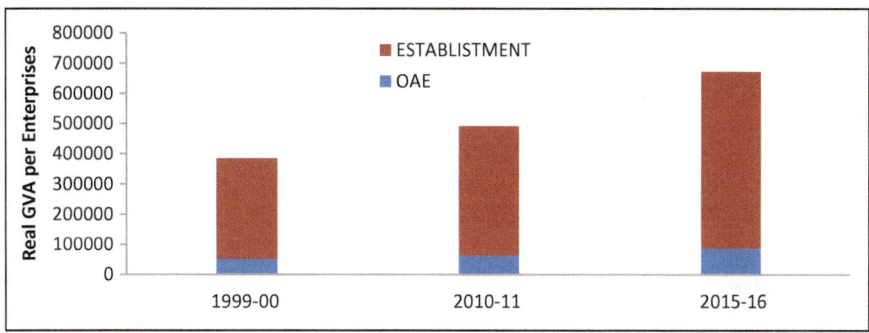

Source: Author Estimation form various Enterprises round of NSSO unit level Data.

Fig. 7.5 Real gross value-added per-enterprises by enterprises type. *Source:* author estimation form various enterprises round of NSSO unit level data

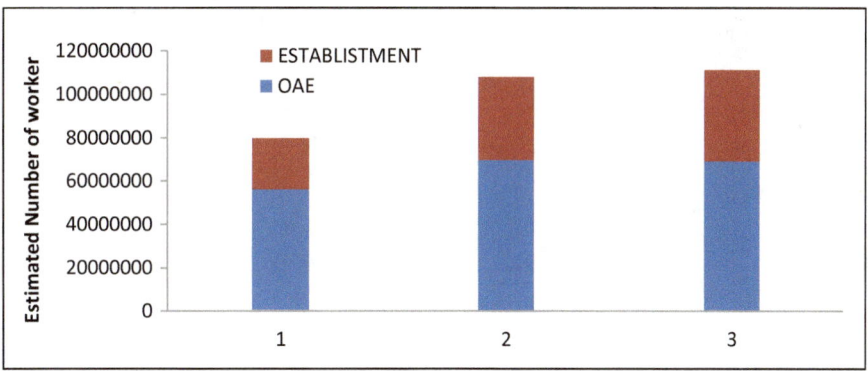

Source: Author Estimation form various Enterprises round of NSSO unit level Data.

Fig. 7.6 Estimated number of worker by enterprises type. *Source:* author estimation form various enterprises round of NSSO unit level data

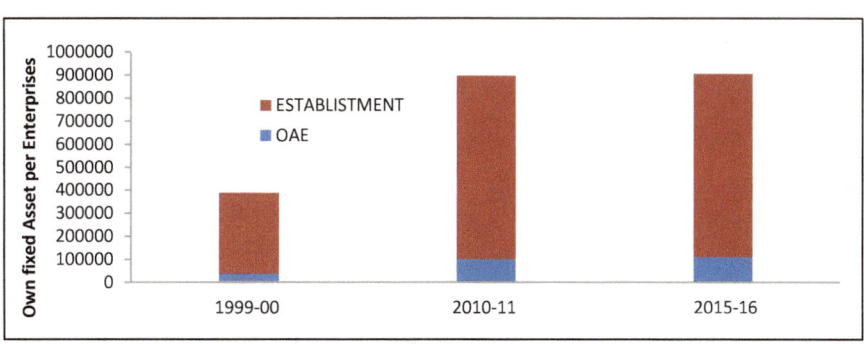

Source: Author Estimation form various Enterprises round of NSSO unit level Data.

Fig. 7.7 Real value of fixed asset per-enterprises by enterprises type. *Source:* author estimation form various enterprises round of NSSO unit level data

Appendix 2

Basic Analysis of Home-Based, Non-Home-Based and Other Enterprises

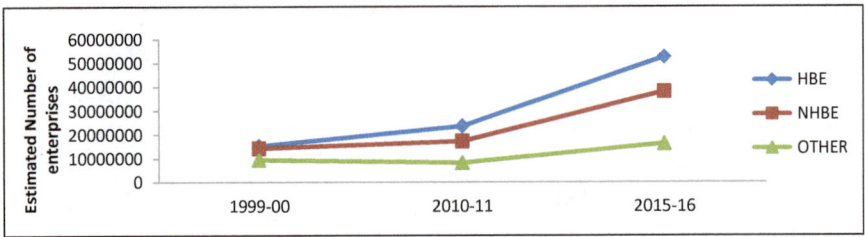

Source: Author Estimation form various Enterprises round of NSSO unit level Data.

Fig. 7.8 Estimated number of enterprises by category of enterprises. *Source:* author estimation form various enterprises round of NSSO unit level data

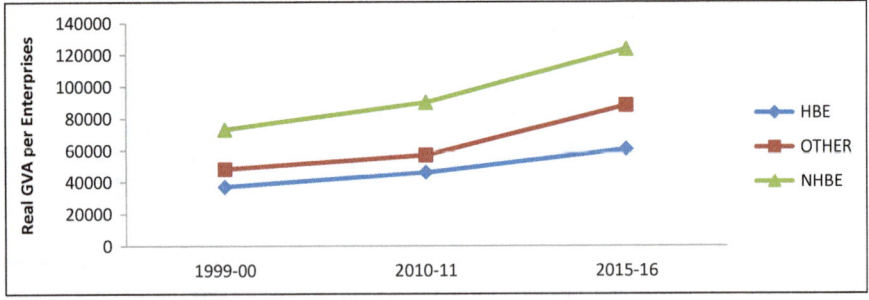

Source: Author Estimation form various Enterprises round of NSSO unit level Data.

Fig. 7.9 Real gross value-added of enterprises by category of enterprises. *Source:* author estimation form various enterprises round of NSSO unit level data

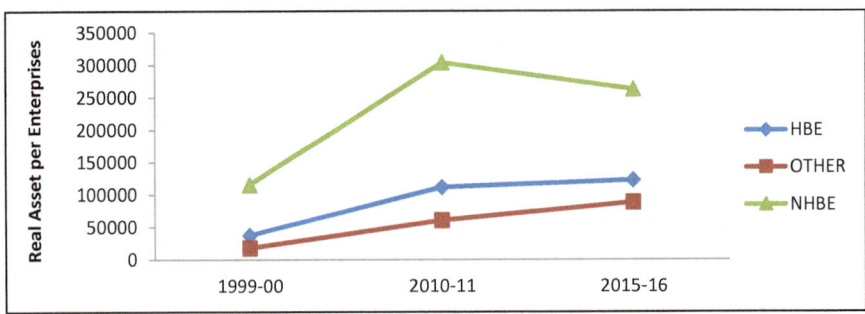

Source: Author Estimation form various Enterprises round of NSSO unit level Data.

Fig. 7.10 Real fixed asset of enterprises by category of enterprises. *Source:* author estimation form various enterprises round of NSSO unit level data

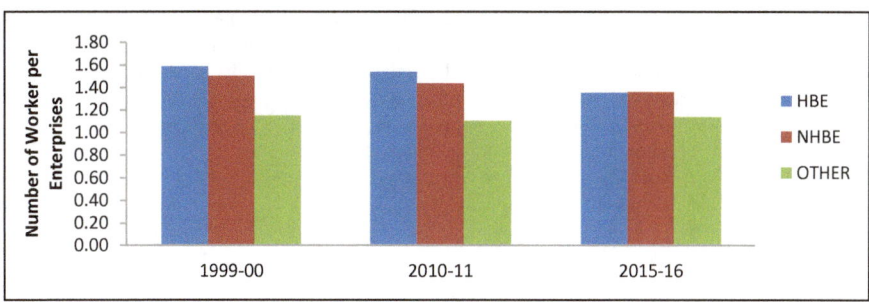

Source: Author Estimation form various Enterprises round of NSSO unit level Data.

Fig. 7.11 Number of worker in enterprises by category of enterprises. *Source:* author estimation form various enterprises round of NSSO unit level data

References

Ahluwalia, I. J. (1991). *Productivity and growth in Indian manufacturing*. New Delhi: Oxford University Press.

Balakrishnan, P., & Pushpangadan, K. (1994). Total factor productivity growth in manufacturing industry a fresh look. *Economic and Political Weekly, 29*, 2028–2035.

Balakrishnan, P., & Pushpangadan, K. (1998). What do we know about productivity growth in Indian industry? *Economic and Political Weekly, 33*, 2241–2246.

Banerjee, N. (1988). Small and large units: Symbiosis or matsyanyaya? In K. B. Suri (Ed.), *Small scale enterprises in industrial development* (pp. 184–202). New Delhi: Sage Publications.

Basant, R., & Chandra, P. (2002). Building technological capabilities in a liberalising developing economy: Firm strategies and public policy. *Economics of Innovation and New Technology, 11* (4–5), 399–421.

Basant, R., & Pankaj, C. (2002). Building technological capabilities in a liberalising developing economy: Firm strategies and public policies. *Economics of Innovation and New Technology, 11*(4/5), 399–421.

Bose, A. N. (1978). *Calcutta and rural Bengal: Small sector symbiosis*. Calcutta: Minerva Associates.

Caves, D. W., Christensen, L. R., & Diewert, D. W. (1982). The economic theory of index numbers and the measurement of input, output and productivity. *Econometrica, 56*(6), 1393–1414.

Chen, E. K. Y. (1979). *Hyper-growth in Asian economies a comparative study of Hong Kong, Japan, Korea, Singapore, and Taiwan*. New York: Holmes & Meier Publishers.

CUTS International. (2003). Competitiveness of Indian informal sector and cottage Industries in the era of globalization and economic liberalization, launch meeting, 9–10 June, 2003. Retrieved form http://www.cuts-international.org/cspac-gelis-workshop.htm#Launch_meet

Davies, R., & Thurlow, J. (2010). Formal–informal economy linkages and unemployment in South Africa. *South African Journal of Economics, 78*(4), 437–459.

Diewert, W. E. (2000). *The quadratic approximation lemma and decompositions of superlative indexes, Discussion Paper 00–15, Department of Economics*. Canada: University of British Columbia.

Fare, R., & Primont, D. (1995). *Multi-output production and duality: Theory and applications*. Netherlands: Kluwer Academic Publishers.

Fare, R., Norris, S. G. M., & Zhang, Z. (1994). Productivity growth, technical progress and efficiency change in industrialised countries. *American Economic Review, 81*(1), 66–83.

Ghani, E., William, R. K., & O'Connell, S. D. (2013). The exceptional persistence of India's unorganized sector, policy research working paper, 6454. World Bank.

Goldar, B. N. (1986). Import substitution, industrial concentration and productivity growth in indian manufacturing. *Oxford Bulletin of Economics and Statistics, 48*(2), 143–164.

Government of India (GOI). (2008). *Report of the independent group on home based worker.* New Delhi: Ministry of Statistics and Programme Implementation.

Griliches, Z., & Ringsted, V. (1971). *Economies of scale and form of the production function.* Amsterdam: North-Holland Publishing Company.

Grosskopf, S. (1986). The role of the reference technology in measuring productive efficiency. *Economic Journal, Royal Economic Society, 96*, 499–513.

Harriss, J. (1982). Character of an urban economy: 'Small scale' production and labour Markets in Coimbatore. *Economic and Political Weekly, 17*(24), 993–1002.

Hart, K. (1973). Informal income opportunities and urban employment in ghana. *The Journal of Modern African Studies, 11*(1), 61–89.

International Labour Organization. (1996). *Home work convention, No. 177.* Retrieved May, 2018, from http://www.ilo.org/ilolex/cgi-lex/convde.pl?c177

International Labour Organization. (2002). *Decent work and the informal economy.* https://www.ilo.org/public/english/standards/relm/ilc/ilc90/pdf/rep-vi.pdf

Kathuria, V., Rajesh, R. S. N., & Sen, K. (2010). Organised versus unorganised manufacturing performance in the post-reform period. *Economic and Political Weekly, 45*(24), 56–75.

Lovell, C. A. K. (1993). Production frontiers and productive efficiency. In H. O. Fried, C. A. K. Lovell, & S. S. Schmidt (Eds.), *The measurement of productivity efficiency—Techniques and applications* (pp. 3–67). New York: Oxford University Press.

Mahadevan, R. (2003). To measure or not to measure total factor productivity growth? *Oxford Development Studies, 31*(3), 365–378.

Mahadevan, R. (2004). *The economics of productivity in Asia and Australia.* Cheltenham: Edward Elgar.

Majumdar, R. (2004). Productivity growth in small enterprises role of inputs, technological progress and learning by doing. *The Indian Journal of Labour Economics, 47*, 901–911.

Marjit, S. (2003). Economic reform and informal wage—A general equilibrium analysis. *Journal of Development Economics, 72*(1), 371–378.

Morris, S., & Basant, R. (2004). Role of small scale industries in the age of liberalisation. In *Asian Development Bank-INRM Policy Brief-11.*

Moser, C. O. N. (1978). Informal sector or petty commodity production: Dualism or dependence in urban development? *World Development, 6*(9–10), 1041–1064.

Natarajan, S., & Rajesh, S. N. R. (2007). *Technical efficiency in the informal manufacturing enterprises: Farm level evidence from the Indian state,* MPRA Working Paper No. 7816.

Portes, A. (2014). Introduction: Immigration and its aftermath. *International Migration Review, 28* (4), 578–598.

Portes, L. A., & Shleifer, A. (2014). Informality and development. *Journal of Economic Perspectives, 28*(3), 123–145.

Rajesh, R. S. N., & Duraisamy, M. (2007). *Economic reforms, efficiency change and productivity growth: An interstate analysis of indian unorganised manufacturing sector,* SSRN Paper.

Rajesh, R. S. N., & Duraisamy, M. (2008). Efficiency and productivity in the Indian unorganised manufacturing sector: Did reform matter? *International Review of Economics, 55*(4), 373–399.

Ranis, G., & Stewart, F. (1999). V-goods and the role of the urban informal sector in development. *Economic Development and Cultural Change, 47*(2), 259–288.

Ray, S. C. (2002). Did indian's economic reforms improve efficiency and productivity? A nonparametric analysis of the initial evidence from manufacturing. *Indian Economic Review, 37*(1), 23–57.

Sahu, P. P. (2010). Subcontracting in india's unorganised manufacturing sector: A mode of adoption or exploitation? *Journal of South Asian Development, 5*(1), 53–83.

Sanyal, K. K. (2007). *Rethinking capitalist development: Primitive accumulation*. Routledge: Governmentality and Post-colonial Capitalism.

Schneider, F., Buehn, A., & Montenegro, C. E. (2010). New estimates for the shadow economies all over the world. *International Economic Journal, 24*(4), 443–461.

Tokman, V. E. (1978). An exploration into the nature of informal – Formal sector relationship. *World Development, 6*(9–10), 1065–1075.

Unel, B. (2003). *Productivity trends in india's manufacturing sectors in the last two decades. IMF Working Paper No. WP/, 03*(22).

Wattanapruttipaisan, T. (2002). SME subcontracting as bridgehead to competitiveness: Framework for an assessment of supply-side capabilities and demandside requirements. *Asia-Pacific Development Journal, 9*(1), 65–87.

Chapter 8
An Analysis of the Trade Relationship of Sri Lanka with Singapore Based on Trade Liberalization

A. A. M. Nufile

8.1 Introduction

Trade is an integral part of economic development and efforts sustaining the national growth of economy and prosperity. This is, in fact, a crucial instrument for industrialization while accessing to foreign exchange is essential for sustainable economic development. The liberal economist always argues that "all countries that had sustained growth and prosperity have opened up their markets to trade and investment". On their views of comparative advantage, liberalizing trade can benefit economically. Some other useful resources such as land, physical, and human capital are to be made sure they can be highly useful at level best.

Sri Lanka's economic growth and development experiences are viewed throughout various periods, especially after the episode of 1977 as it is more important than before. During that period, the government has implemented many development strategies and framed policies as well as they were turning to Sri Lanka's economy. The dimension of those policies and strategies varies more than before (Balakrishnan 2010, pp. 15–16).

The government's new policy has included flexibility on dominancy, restrictions or control and intervention, and followed liberal policy, relaxation of interest rate, strengthening market oriented, ownership, privatization, foreign investment, export oriented industrialization, and outlook development. Now, the economic liberalization policy is 35 years old. During this long period, the development and economic growth experiences and effects of the liberalization vary on large scales.

A. A. M. Nufile (✉)
Department of Economics and Statistics, South Eastern University of Sri Lanka, Oluvil, Sri Lanka
e-mail: nufile68@seu.ac.lk

© The Author(s), under exclusive license to Springer Nature Switzerland AG 2021   123
A. K. Mishra et al. (eds.), *Advances in Innovation, Trade and Business*,
Contributions to Management Science,
https://doi.org/10.1007/978-3-030-60354-0_8

Nowadays, the system of trade has come to be seen in a two ways. One is that of the international trade and other one is regional pattern of trade or called as intra-regional trade. Based on this point of view, the first one is indicating the mutual transaction of tradable goods and services taking place between the two countries for a long period of time. Next one is the transactions of goods and services between regional or intra-regional setup as well as neighboring countries which made it under the special circumstances (Nufile 2006).

8.2 Literature Review

It examines empirical research on the economic effect of regionalism based on the trade liberalization. The original study of the Jacob Viner (1950) contributes illustratively the possibilities of the trade creation and trade diversion effect through the formation of the custom union. Further, the above study divides empirical approaches into four categories: one is partial equilibrium analysis, second is general equilibrium analysis, third is gravity model approaches, and the fourth is ex-post studies of regionalism.

According to Ariffin (2007), the first and second model-based counterfactual analyses while they involve either perfectly or imperfectly competitive markets. The third group of study originally developed by Jan Tinbergen (1962) with the reason of analyzing determinants of bilateral trade flows between partners. Fourth one is followed by de la Torre and Kelly (1992).

Original empirical studies have been done over the years to calculate the economic and welfare effects of regional trading arrangement (RTAs). This type of study started soon after Viner's (1950) vital contribution in theoretical impact of trade diversion effect due to the formation of custom union. Thereafter Verdoorn (1954), Janseen (1961), and Krause (1963) also contributed to the study of the economic effects on regionalism. Balassa (1967) also pointed out their significant role in examining the custom union in his study. Originally under Viner's outline, trade creation is linked with the expansion of trade between partner countries in agreement with comparative advantage.

These researches carried out by Waqif and Chatterjee (1993), Ahuja and Bhattacharya (1993), Reddy (1993), Shrestha (1993), Thapa 1993, Wanigaratne (1993), and Yapa (1993) belong to the primary stage. These researches reveal the advantages obtained by the co-operation in the fields of agriculture, energy, manufacturing, and services through the inflow of investment with intra-regional trade. Furthermore, the limitation of economic and organizational constrains found among intra-regional economic co-operation of SAARC have been compared with that of European Union. Besides, it has been pointed out in these researches that, through regional arrangement, the increase in welfare will occur and it is inevitable that a SAARC member country continues to maintain the trade relationship with a third country.

Srinivasan and Canonero (1993), Srinivasan (1994) maintain that South Asian countries could obtain innumerable benefits through their regional co-operation and regional trade extension. The conclusion of research reached by them states that small economy of SAARC countries have contributed remarkably to the intra-regional trade development. That is to say that, trade extension has taken place comparatively in small economy more than big economy. But, according to Das (2001) big economic countries like India and Pakistan did not have a considerable trade-creation effect.

Nufile (2019) has studied to examine the trade relationship of Sri Lanka with Bangladesh after trade liberalization enforced in Sri Lanka after year 1977 by using quantitative approach. The time series data from 1980 to 2015 were used in his gravity regression model. Further, he has carried out his work through the dependent variable which is the value of total bilateral trade between Sri Lanka and Bangladesh. The independent variables of the model are defined as Per capita GDP, Total trade-GDP ratio (Openness ratio), Inflation, Exchange rate of both countries, and South Asia Free Trade Agreement. The research found that free trade system could be able to change Sri Lanka's regional trade after Sri Lanka's liberalization.

8.3   Objective of the Study

The objective of this study is to examine the trade relationship of Sri Lanka with Singapore after trade liberalization in year 1977.

8.4   Methodology

It explains the sources of data and explains the coverage of this study that runs over a period of 38 years, from 1980 to 2018. This study covers a total of 02 countries. These countries are chosen on the basis of importance of trading partnership with Sri Lanka and availability of required data. Data used in this part of research cover a period of 38 years (1980–2018) after the trade liberalization in Sri Lanka. The two countries such as Sri Lanka and Singapore are analyzed in this study to achieve the objective of this study.

For this objective, a regression analysis of the gravity model is used as follows:

$$
\begin{aligned}
\text{Log } T_{ij} = {} & \beta_0 + \beta_1 \log \left(\text{PCGDP}_{ij} \right) + \beta_2 \log \left(\text{TR}_i / \text{GDP}_i \right) \\
& + \beta_3 \log \left(\text{TR}_{ij} / \text{GDP}_j \right) + \beta_4 \log \left(\text{IF}_{ij} \right) + \qquad \beta_5 \log \left(\text{ER}_{ij} \right) \\
& + \beta_6 \log \left(\text{IEF}_{ij} \right) + \in_{ij}
\end{aligned} \tag{8.1}
$$

where

T_{ij} = total bilateral trade (US $) between Sri Lanka and country j (Singapore) at t time,

$PCGDP_{ij}$ = per capita GDP (US $) of Sri Lanka and country j (Singapore) at t time,

TR_i/GDP_i = trade-GDP ratio [openness (US $)] of Sri Lanka at t time,

TR_{ij}/GDP_j = total bilateral trade-GDP ratio [openness (US $)] of country ij (Singapore) at t time,

IF_{ij} = inflation (GDP Deflator) annual percentage of Sri Lanka and country j (Singapore) at t time,

ER_{ij} = nominal exchange rate of Sri Lanka and country j (Singapore) at t time,

IEF_{ij} = index of economic freedom of country i and country j (Singapore) at t time,

$\in_{ij}$ = error term, and β_0, β_1, β_2, β_3, β_4 β_5, β_6, and β_7 = parameters.

8.5   Analysis and Findings

8.5.1   The Effects of Free Trade on Sri Lanka's Bilateral Trade with Singapore

The objective of this study is to examine how the trade of Sri Lanka and Singapore as member of SAARC/SAFTA has been carried out during the period of study (1980–2018). This study analyses the trade patterns of Sri Lanka with Singapore to examine how the trade has changed, especially post-economic liberalization period of Sri Lanka. Thus, this study is to examine the trade relationship of Sri Lanka with Singapore.

8.5.1.1   Sri Lanka–Singapore Bilateral Trade

The importance of region of the ASEAN countries has been taken as the second effort to make out the characters of determining factors of Sri Lanka's bilateral trade. However, the countries are considered in alphabetical order which is systematically simplified. Therefore, the fifth is Singapore that is an AFTA member country which is used to estimate the relationship between selected variables and intra-regional trade. Table 8.1 explains the trade directions between Singapore and Sri Lanka (Figs. 8.1 and 8.2). The exports of Sri Lanka to Singapore and the imports of Sri Lanka form Singapore and the exports of Singapore to Sri Lanka and the imports of Singapore from Sri Lanka ranging from year 1980 to year 2018 are vividly depicted in Table 8.1.

Table 8.1 Sri Lanka–Singapore bilateral trades (1980–2018) values in US $ million

| Year | Sri Lanka (01) | | Singapore (02) | |
	Exports (to Singapore)	Imports (from Singapore)	Exports (to Sri Lanka)	Imports (from Sri Lanka)
1980	11.8	91.3	159	18
1985	45.9	73.7	193	43
1990	45.0	103	222	33
1995	73.0	250	377	54
1996	60.0	258	387	51
1997	58.0	286	398	47
1998	44.0	311	524	48
1999	44.54	451.77	465	38
2000	61.00	496.02	461	55
2001	57.12	410.43	396	33
2002	72.25	431.96	382	50
2003	65.86	522.20	485	52
2004	86.48	698.45	592	74
2005	79.39	736.86	681	59
2006	74.70	992.75	922	53
2007	80.46	1107.12	836	70
2008	76.99	1600.63	989	71
2009	87.83	1116.7	761	76
2010	513.33	1614.97	1199	87
2011	406.42	1534.5	1333	142
2012	93.43	1275.3	1564	83
2013	103.17	1804.6	1965	141
2014	140.13	1270.62	1751	109
2015	78.05	922.53	1381	107
2016	107.82	1030.69	1310	88
2017	191.37	1292.7	1827	129
2018	153.25	1411.38	1785	95

Sources: IMF (1987–2019), "Direction of Trade Statistics Year Book"

8.5.1.2 Sri Lanka–Singapore Bilateral Trade

The following multiple regression model of log–log has been used in this study and this is the best model selected based on various model selection statistics.

$$\text{Log } T_{ij} = \beta_0 + \beta_1 \left(\text{PCGDP}_{ij}\right) + \beta_2 (\text{TR}_i/\text{GDP}_i) + \beta_3 \left(\text{TR}_{ij}/\text{GDP}_j\right) \\ + \beta_4 \left(\text{IF}_{ij}\right) + \beta_5 \left(\text{ER}_{ij}\right) + \beta_6 \left(\text{IEF}_{ij}\right) + \in_{ij} \tag{8.2}$$

According to the values of all model selection statistics, adjusted R square, "F" value and VIF are very good in all models. But "F" value is not sufficient in only linear-log model. However, VIF value is very good in linear-linear and log-linear

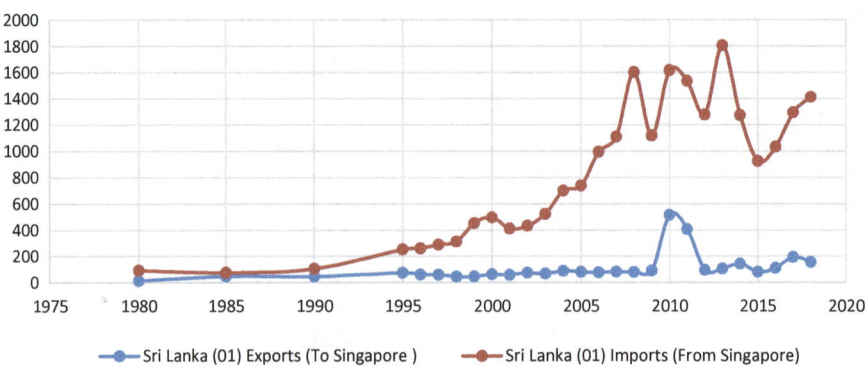

Fig. 8.1 Sri Lanka's trade with Singapore (1980–2018)

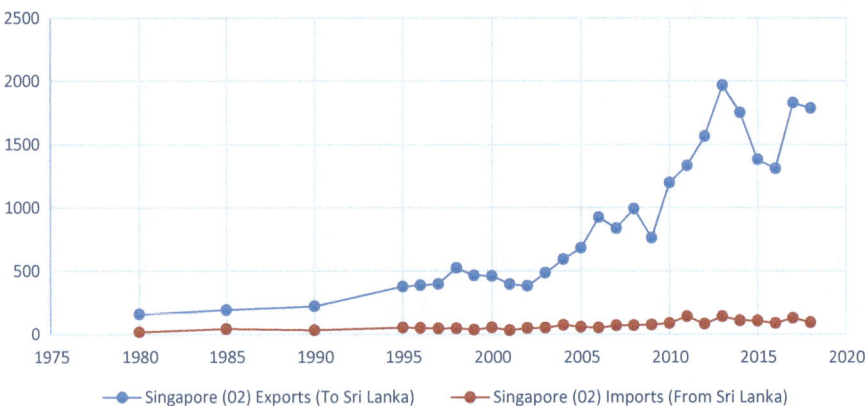

Fig. 8.2 Singapore's trade with Sri Lanka (1980–2018)

models and other two models like log–log and linear–log models have a problem. Further, Variance-Inflating Factor (VIF) is estimated between 1.2 and 13.9 in all the models. It indicates that there is serious multi-co-linearity among the variables in log–log and linear–log models.

But, since the value of Durbin–Watson (DW) d statistic has been estimated at $d_L = 1.14674 \leq DW \geq d_U = 2.29259$, three models such as log–linear, log–log, and linear-log are situated between the zone of not rejecting area. However, the linear-linear model consists of the zone of indecision area. Therefore, log-linear model has been selected because there is no autocorrelation among the error observation ($\alpha = 0.01$). Further, all these values are very good in log-linear model. Therefore, the log-linear model is accepted for Sri Lanka–Singapore trade test completion.

According to Table 8.2, signs of all variables are as expected in the theoretical or hypothetical argument. Regression results show that TR_i/GDP_{it}, TR_{ijt}/GDP_{jt}, IF_{ij}, and IEF_{ijt} are statistically highly significant to determine the bilateral trade of Sri Lanka with Singapore. However, the variables such as Per capita Income and

Table 8.2 Regression results for the log–linear model of post-liberalization period (1980–2018) (influence factors on Sri Lanka–Singapore bilateral trade)

"Predictor/variables"	"Coefficient"	"Probability"
Constant	19.942	0.000***
$PCGDP_{ijt}$	−0.00000002	0.376
TR_i/GDP_{it}	3.3685	0.000***
TR_{ijt}/GDP_{jt}	0.31577	0.000***
IF_{ijt}	−0.002914	0.030**
ER_{ijt}	0.02843	0.450
IEF_{ijt}	−0.0019367	0.000***

Note: Estimated $\alpha = 0.1^*$; 0.05^{**}; 0.01^{***}

Exchange Rate do not affect the bilateral trade of both countries. Though the two factors such as $TR_i/GDPit$ and TR_{ijt}/GDP_{jt} are positively influencing on the bilateral trade, other two variables such as Inflation and Index of Economic Freedom are negatively affecting the bilateral trade of the two countries. The results show that all the estimated coefficients are highly statistically significant because their p values are either zero or extremely small.

The estimated coefficients are interpreted as follows. The trade to GDP ratio is 3.3685, meaning that, if trade to GDP ratio goes up by 1 unit, the bilateral trade goes up by 3.36%, holding other variables constant. So, the openness of unilateral trade has facilitated to both countries for the expansion of bilateral trade. While Intra-Trade Ratio goes up by 1 unit, the bilateral trade goes up by 0.31% holding other variables constant. While the inflation goes up by 1 unit, bilateral trade goes down by 0.29%. Hence, inflation factor hits the bilateral trade negatively.

The index of economic freedom is also negatively (−0.0019367) influencing on bilateral trade, that is, the coefficient of IEF_{ijt} tells us that as IEF_{ijt} goes up 1 unit, bilateral trade goes down by 0.19%. It clearly explains that unilateral economic freedom (Singapore as a first rank of the country at IEF_{ijt} in the world) never helps Sri Lanka. Here, the free trade system could be able to change Sri Lanka's regional trade after Sri Lanka's liberalization.

8.6   Summary and Conclusions

There is a clear proof from the results that the trade liberalization is more helpful to Sri Lanka for her bilateral trade expansion or increase with SAARC member countries. But, individually, the per capita Gross Domestic Product (GDP) differs as larger among them. Singapore is consisting of large number of population in comparison with Sri Lanka. Thus, Sri Lanka tried to have more exports through the free trade agreement. The matter of inflation was cut down by the bilateral trade. And also, the practice of existing economic freedom did not support to both countries. Thus, Sri Lanka tried to have more exports through the free trade agreement. The both countries benefited through the meaningful achievement from the operation of existing economic freedom.

References

Ahuja, S., & Bhattacharya, R. (1993). SAARC-ASEAN trade complementarities and regional import substitution prospects. In A. Waqif (Ed.), *Economic and sectoral co-operation in south Asia*. New Delhi: Friedrich Ebert Foundation.

Ariffin, A. (2007*), The free trade doctrine, the ASEAN free trade area and their effect on trade and trade policy*, Unpublished Thesis, Murdoch Business School, Australia, Murdoch University.

Balakrishnan, N. (2010). *Development problems in Sri Lankan economy*. Colombo, Sri Lanka: Kumaran Press, ISBN: 978-955-659-240-5.

Balassa, B. (1967). Trade creation and trade diversion in the European common market. *Economic Journal, 77*(305), 1–21.

Das, D. K. (2001). Regionalism in a globalizing world: An Asia-Pacific perspective, *CSGR Working Paper*, No-80/01, UK, Centre for the Study of Globalization and Regionalization. Retrieved from, http://www.csgr.org.

de la Torre, A., & Kelly, M. (1992). *Regional trading arrangement, IMF: Occasional Paper, No: 93*. Washington, DC: International Monetary Fund.

Janseen, L. H. (1961). *Free trade, protection and customs union*. Leiden: H. E. Stenfert Kroese.

Krause (1963). European economic integration and the United States, AEA, *American Economic Review*, Papers and Proceeding, May (pp 185–196).

Nufile, A. A. (2019). An analysis of the trade relationship of Sri Lanka with Bangladesh after trade liberalization, South Eastern University of Sri Lanka. *Journal of Business Economics, 18*(3), 78–82.

Nufile, A. M. (2006). *SAARC: Intra-regional trade and its impact on member countries: Special reference to Sri Lanka*, Unpublished Thesis, Peradeniya-Sri Lanka, Department of Economics, University of Peradeniya.

Reddy, M. J. (1993). Indo-Canadian trade and implications for economic co-operation. In A. Waqif (Ed.), *Economic and sectoral co-operation in South Asia*. New Delhi: Friedrich Ebert Foundation.

Shrestha, P. R. (1993). Economic perspectives and regional co-operation. In A. Waqif (Ed.), *Economic and sectoral co-operation in South Asia*. New Delhi: Friedrich Ebert Foundation.

Srinivasan, T. N. (1994). *Regional trading arrangement and beyond: Exploring some options for South Asia: Theory, empirics and policy*, Report no: IDP-142, South Asia Region, World Bank.

Srinivasan, T. N., & Canonero, G. (1993). *Liberalization of trade among Neighbours: Two illustrative models and simulations*, South Asia Region Discussion Paper Series, Supplement II to IDP No: 142.

Thapa, A. N. S. (1993). Areas of co-operation in specific economic sectors and commodities. In A. Waqif (Ed.), *Economic and sectoral co-operation in South Asia*. New Delhi: Friedrich Ebert Foundation.

Tinbergen, J. (1962). An analysis of world trade flows-suggestions for an international policy. In J. Tinbergen (Ed.), *Shaping the world economy*. New York: The Twentieth Century Fund.

Verdoorn, P. J. (1954). A customs union for Western Europe-advantages and feasibility. *World Politics, 6*, 482–500.

Viner, J. (1950), The customs union issue, CEIP, New York-Sri Lanka, Carnegie Endowment for International Peace.

Wanigaratne, R. A. M. C. (1993). Investment co-operation in South Asia- is it possible? In A. Waqif (Ed.), *Economic and sectoral co-operation in South Asia*. New Delhi: Friedrich Ebert Foundation.

Waqif, A. A., & Chatterjee, A. (1993). Economic and sectoral co-operation in South Asia. In A. Waqif (Ed.), *Economic and sectoral co-operation in South Asia*. New Delhi: Friedrich Ebert Foundation.

Yapa, L. F. (1993). Co-operative development and promotion of exports—A Sri Lankan perspective. In A. Waqif (Ed.), *Economic and sectoral co-operation in South Asia*. New Delhi: Friedrich Ebert Foundation.

Index

A
Anti-dumping duty, 59, 65, 67
ASEAN-6, 57–67

B
Banking sector development (BSD), 35–44

C
Capital intensity, 70–72, 76–81, 102, 103, 105,
    106, 113

D
Demography, 87

E
Efficiency, 2–9, 11, 15, 16, 18–28, 70–72, 80,
    95–116
Exports, 1, 2, 4, 6–8, 10, 13, 14, 20, 22, 29, 61,
    73, 77–81, 88, 95, 123, 126, 127, 129

F
Firm performance, 70–73, 75–80
Firm size, 70, 71, 75, 77–81
Foreign direct investment (FDI), 35–44, 47–55,
    85–93

G
Granger causality, 36–38, 41, 43, 44

Gravity models, 1–3, 5, 11, 12, 15, 124, 125
Gravity regression model, 125
Gross domestic product (GDP), 10, 13, 14, 24,
    25, 28, 36, 38, 41–44, 85–91, 93, 96,
    125, 126, 129

H
Home-based enterprises (HBE), 95–116

I
India, 3, 10, 14–20, 22, 24, 25, 29, 47–55,
    57–65, 67, 69–82, 87, 95–116, 125
Intellectual property rights (IPR), 48–54, 79

M
Manufacturing firms, 47–55, 71, 74
MSMEs, 69–80

O
Own account enterprises (OAE), 96, 97, 113

P
Productivity, 1–3, 6, 7, 18, 22, 35, 70, 72, 73,
    95–116

R
R&D, 48, 50, 51, 55, 70, 72, 76–81
Reforms, 1–12, 14–16, 18–28, 44, 48, 101, 113

© The Author(s), under exclusive license to Springer Nature Switzerland AG 2021
A. K. Mishra et al. (eds.), *Advances in Innovation, Trade and Business*,
Contributions to Management Science,
https://doi.org/10.1007/978-3-030-60354-0

S
Singapore, 4, 7, 58, 60–64, 123–129
Sri Lanka, 3, 12, 14, 15, 17, 18, 21, 28,
      123–129
Stochastic frontier, 1–3, 5, 11, 12

T
Technological activities, 50
Trade diversion, 59, 60, 67, 124
Trade dynamics, 1, 2, 7, 28
Trade liberalization, 25, 123–130

U
Unit roots, 38–41, 43, 89–91

V
Vector autoregression (VAR), 41, 43, 85–93

W
West Africa, 35–45